Jack Kain
JJCPRN S. 18-19

neighborhood, church, job, and international setting. Only the truth of the Holy Scriptures reveals a global cure for being 'my brother's keeper.'"

~Dr. Darnell Johnson, Former Chaplain
Southern Correctional Ministries, Hampton, VA

"My Brother's Keeper is a testimony that what is learned so early in life can make such a difference globally if we trust God to order our steps. From deception to deployment, we must teach our children to love and reconcile their differences. Each one teach one for world peace."

~Dr. Stephanie D. B. Johnson
Principal, Early Childhood Education

"The principles of biblical reconciliation with very powerful real-life examples of its practical application are the essentials of what makes this book required reading for anyone seeking God's direction for healing and restitution from the unimaginable destruction of history's most deplorable examples of man's inhumanity against man."

~Rev. Ronald V. Myers, Sr., M.D.
Founder & Chairman
National Day of Reconciliation
and Healing from the Legacy of Enslavement
National Juneteenth Christian Leadership
Council (NJCLC)

"Warring and death began with man. People have to be made aware of the need for reconciliation. We must tell what Jesus paid the price for. We must be our brother's keeper and not his killer. Global reconciliation depends on it."

~Dr. George W. Thomas
Minister,
Businessman, and Missionary
on the 1987 South African trip

JACK GAINES

MY BROTHER'S KEEPER NOT MY BROTHER'S KILLER

RECONCILIATION: THE GLOBAL
TOOL FOR RESTORATION

First Edition

The author is grateful for permission to include the following
previously copyrighted material:
Unless otherwise indicated, all Scripture quotations are taken from
The New King James Version. Copyright © 1979, 1980, 1982,
Thomas Nelson, Inc.
Scripture quotations marked NIV are taken frm *The Holy Bible: New
International Version*® NIV ® . Copyright © 1973, 1978, 1984 by
International Bible Society.
Used by permission of Zondervan Publishing House.
All rights reserved

Gaines, Jack.
My Brother's Keeper Not My Brother's Killer / Reconciliation:
The Global Tool for Restoration / by Jack Gaines.

ISBN 978-0-944391-00-6
1. Reconciliation. 2. Genocide 3. Religions 4. Causation

Design: Don Wise Productions, Inc.
Cover Photo: D. Wise: Most assuredly, I say unto you, unless a grain of wheat
fall into the ground and dies, it remains alone: but if it dies, it bears much fruit.
Pencil Sketch: R. Zimmerman

HIS PATH PUBLISHING
A DIVISION OF
ForWord, LLC
P.O. Box 9708
Chesapeake, VA 23321
www.hispath.us

Printed in the United States of America

To Ma and Dad

You gave us so much of your time,
your energy—yourselves—
that we might know the difference
between "looking" and "seeing,"
the "material" and the "spiritual."
Thank you for believing in us
and introducing us to God
at such an early age.
Thank you, also, for being
perfect examples of those
who would truly be
their brother's keepers.
We never knew anyone
that you would not help.
We will never forget.

CONTENTS

ACKNOWLEDGMENTS

Among the many who contributed to the fulfillment of this process, I would like to thank my family—my wife and my children—who proved to be such a source of encouragement to me throughout this project. My own parents, too, would be so proud to know that their combined efforts in raising all of us (my four siblings and I) have ultimately contributed something significant to this world (just as they repeatedly implored us to do). I extend gratitude to "Pastor Mac" (along with his church) that helped start me on this long journey. Finally, I would like to thank the unusual team of individuals (my brother, Jerry, Donna, Ann, Don, and Chris) who, despite their differences in age, race, and cultural upbringing, came together and allowed God to reveal to each of us that He can, indeed, take the various gifts of any number of people,and make it all work to His glory. Each of us is convinced not only that none of it was mere coincidence, but that it was a miracle in itself. In the end, it is my great hope that an understanding of the truths within these pages will move the people of this world—individuals and couples, churches and organizations, races and tribes, governments and nations—to live in the Reconciled Paradigm that is unfolded herein.

FOREWORD

The true pathway to peace and reconciliation is here unfolded by Jack Gaines. It leads to freedom and growth instead of the self-imposed prison created by hatred. Forgiveness is at the core of this peace-building paradigm. But can this process work for nations? Is it not just another religious discourse?

Jack Gaines's response is quite striking as he states: *"The world is searching for peace, but peace is not in the DNA of man."*

Most of the time in history and even today, religions have fueled hatred or prevented countries from reaching peace. This book is not about religion; it is about understanding the deep roots of our inability, as humans, to achieve peace and reconciliation.

Jack Gaines's personal experience as well as his search for peace has led to some groundbreaking revelations. And I have been privileged to meet him in his journey and to partake with him in the process which led, in 1999, to the organization of "The Leaders Conference for Reconciliation & Development" in Cotonou (Benin Republic).

Feelings of hurt inspire retaliation and claim for compensation: and here is the trap of bitterness where we cherish the status of being victimized. Whereas the Bible says, *"No, in all these things we are more than conquerors through Him who loved us"* (Romans 8:37, NIV).

The treatments inflicted upon the victims are officially reported in the historical records, mostly with distortions to favor the views and interests of those who still want to find a legal ground for their iniquities. So the prevailing "truth" is indeed a biased record of what has truly happened. But we believe that no one can extend forgiveness if truth is not acknowledged in the first place. But who is the first to acknowledge the truth? "The victim," says Jack Gaines, as he recalls that "God's plan requires <u>the victim to initiate forgiveness</u>, freeing the perpetrator to feel remorse and apologize."

A victim has the responsibility to understand what really happened, in order to initiate forgiveness, for his own sake and restoration!

But forgiveness is hardly seen on Nations' agendas or on the Inter-national Community's agenda for peace-building, with very few exceptions such as the well-known South African post-apartheid Commission for Truth and Reconciliation, thanks to the leadership of Nelson Mandela and Desmond Tutu.

"Forgiveness is the economy of the heart... forgiveness saves the expense of anger, the cost of hatred, the waste of spirits."[1]

This paradigm has never been considered among all the means and powers used in search of peace and security in the world. If only we could reassess our strategies towards this goal in the light of the pathway unveiled here by Jack Gaines, the power of forgiveness will unite millions of souls and bring forth or enhance development in so many parts of the world.

To extend forgiveness to others is "to turn failure into opportunities for growth"[2] for individuals, their communities, and their nations. Here lies the leadership factor. A Peace and Reconciliation Building Process require a leadership filled with the courage to embrace the pathway of true forgiveness.

If you want to know more about God's template for peace, reconciliation, and development for people and nations; if you have never considered the possibility that "God is the enemy of man," and if you desire to step into other striking revelations, this book is for you.

Luc Gnacadja
Assistant Secretary General
Executive Secetary of the
United Nations Convention to
Combat Desertification

[1]Hannah More.
[2]Bill Perkins, "Awaken the Leader Within."

INTRODUCTION

At ten years of age, I often wondered why we, as a people, had to come to America as slaves. I used to go back into the fields behind my house, fold down the waist-high weeds, and carefully clear a place for myself. There I would shut out the world, lie down with my arms folded behind my head, making shapes out of the clouds, and talk to God about all the things that concerned me. This began my own quiet relationship with my Creator. As I grew older and became more inquisitive about life, I went to Him more and more often with my questions.

In my home I was fortunate to have parents who demonstrated respect for all people—for "who they were," not for the color of their skin. Though in 1955 segregation was still widely practiced, my parents seemed to get along well with everyone. At the time the whites in close proximity lived, quite literally, "on the other side of the tracks" from us. For the most part, they stayed on one side of the railroad tracks that divided our community, and we stayed on the other.

Some of the white kids used to come over on our side, though, and we'd play together for hours. Sometimes Ma and Dad would counsel a white lady who shared how her husband would get drunk and beat her. She found security at our house and at the little country store that my dad owned. (There seemed to be at least one of those stores in every traditionally black neighborhood.) As a result we were exposed to white people early on in our lives, and we developed great relationships. Color was never a problem that I could tell.

As my brothers and sisters and I grew older, we could see things beginning to change. Before those changes brought their usual negative effects, my dad (still a young man himself) created a playground behind our house for the black kids who had no real place to play. The playground was replete with chin-up bars, swings, and even a "sprinkler system," actually just a garden hose attached to an outdoor faucet to spray water into the air. It was great on the long, hot days of summer.

I remember especially those chin-up bars. I helped my daddy build them from trees he cut down on our back lot. As a five-year-old child, I was instructed to pick up one of the smaller trees and drag it to the house. When I dropped it halfway there, Daddy prompted, "Pick it up, boy! That tree can't think!" The Gaineses never quit.

My dad also organized the neighborhood Fathers' Club, which formed two Little League baseball teams—the Hawks and the Eagles. He even solicited funds from some of the downtown merchants who invested in uniforms for us, with the names of the donors embroidered on the backs of the jerseys. Our teams played every Saturday during the summer. Parents (some who didn't have children on either team) would come from all around to watch us. When two of our little white friends from across the tracks, Frankie and Herbie, asked to play with us, Daddy put one of them on the Hawks' team and the other on the Eagles'. But when they said that they preferred to play on the same team, he just shrugged and let them do that too.

Whenever we had an away game, we took the best players from both teams and went to play whoever was scheduled. Once, when we were supposed to play a team from another one of the black communities in town, the opposing coaches told us that Herbie and Frankie couldn't come along, but my dad brought them anyway. In the late fifties, nobody ever heard of whites and blacks playing together on the same team. When the other team saw we had brought Herbie and Frankie along, they insisted that they could not participate. My dad simply responded, "If they don't play, we don't play."

My daddy took a stand that day. He packed up his baseball team—his little boys (black and white)—and we went home. "Boys," he said on the way back, "there ain't nothin' like being on a good team." So we stuck together, no matter what, for the rest of that season and several more to come.

Because of my dad's example, I never really saw myself growing up as any different from anyone else. With him as my coach in life as well as in baseball, I felt I could do just about anything. I thought I was pretty good in baseball and my dad agreed, but a dream came true when a talent scout spotted me in a try-out camp in Newport News, Virginia.

The scout walked up behind me on the mound and asked me to throw a curve ball. The pitch was so hard and so fast that when he saw it, he turned, walked all the way to second base, came back to the mound and said, "Throw that again." I knew I had him then. Three days later, he offered me a contract to pitch for the Pittsburgh Pirates. I was seventeen years old.

Since I was underage, my dad had to sign with me. We were invited to the hotel where the scout was staying for the signing. My friends were so excited that they tagged along, but had to stay outside in the car. Both Daddy and I were thrilled that I would be playing for a professional baseball team. At the time neither of us realized that the offer—a sum of $350 a month, almost the amount he was bringing home from his job at the shipyard—was nowhere near the $2,500 or more white pitchers were offered. We did notice right away that we were in the wrong place!

While we were talking, the phone kept ringing. We found out later that it was the hotel manager, informing the scout that complaints had been coming in from other guests about the carload of black people in the parking lot. "Bad for business," he insisted. We left soon after the last call.

Oh, it wasn't that I didn't know whites got special treatment. That's just the way it was in those days. During the six weeks of spring training, black players were not allowed to eat with the other players. We were housed separately too. Then there were the hecklers. Even though I knew I was a good pitcher, the crowds in the stands were not always appreciative. In fact, I recall one night when one guy just wouldn't let up. "Hey, Sambo!" he yelled. "Whatcha doin' out there? Get that uniform off the mound!"

He continued his litany of name-calling until I decided I'd had enough. Since I couldn't get to him, of course, I decided to make every batter pay. We went on to shut out the rest of the line-up. I must admit that I left the mound with a satisfied grin on my face. That night, I learned to take the negatives in life and turn them into positive energy. With adrenaline pumping, I took the league lead in strikeouts, earned run average, and pitched a 2-0 shutout.

I don't suppose I fully grasped the significance of what was going on in society until one day during a game in Greeneville, South Carolina, after I had signed with the Boston Red Sox. I had run over to the sideline to catch a pop-up foul when I noticed some children, their fingers stuck through the fence, screaming, "Ni****!" over and over. Rather than making me mad, the scenario only saddened me. What would cause such animosity in ones so young? It was a question that would haunt me for the rest of my life.

The issue that day, as well as the day my daddy took his Little League team home, was not really about race. It was about what is right and fair. I didn't realize it then, but my father was modeling for me what it meant to be his brother's keeper. Not only did he "keep" the hearts of Herbie and Frankie for a time, but he showed all of us how to find the right pathway and helped me take the first step on my long journey toward reconciliation.

The book you are about to read is not the opinion of one man. It is not an hypothesis, a limited perspective, or a point of view. It is an old, old story—*the* old, old story. It is eternal reality, and if everyone in the world would abide by the simple principles set forth herein, there would be an end to global conflict.

REGARDLESS OF HOW ADVERSE OR UNJUST YOUR SITUATION MIGHT BE, THERE IS ALWAYS A LESSON TO BE LEARNED. AND IT ALL BOILS DOWN TO HOW YOU CHOOSE TO PROCESS IT.

BROTHERS KILLING BROTHERS

WE NEED TO BE RECONCILED TO ONE ANOTHER

"Thou shalt not kill…"

EXODUS 20:13 KJV

"Thou shalt love thy neighbor as thyself."

LEVITICUS 19:18 KJV

He gripped the handle of the knife, then plunged the blade into the old woman's fragile flesh...one, two, three times! Even when his hands were covered with her blood, he didn't stop. Four...five...six more times he attacked. She was the only one standing between him and his next fix...and he needed that fix bad! Now he was slashing wildly, mindlessly, hypnotically...his brain numb to what he was doing. An eighty-four-year-old lifelong neighbor, who had actually gotten up to make him a cup of tea...it didn't matter. He wasn't thinking anymore...except that she kept looking up at him with those pale, pleading eyes...she wouldn't die! Not until he had stabbed her twenty-one times...

This mental image, formed while

ministering to an eighteen-year-old man on his way to Death Row, has never left me. How could someone descend to such an animalistic level that he could violate the helpless? What deep darkness lurks in the human heart so that it can spring suddenly and out of control to destroy the innocent? Why do people kill each other? Age-old questions that beg an answer. Questions that I have been asking God since my childhood—throughout my pro baseball career, a stint in the Army, and fourteen years of prison ministry.

This man's addiction—his desire to have what he wanted, when he wanted it, the way he wanted it—led to a heinous act that has been mirrored in the death of innocents everywhere in the world. Why is it that we choose conflict, confrontation, and violence to solve our problems?

God's Ambassador

In 1994, I met a Rwandan major, who was also a chaplain, at a Regent University conference. While attending this conference, I was privileged to meet many military officers from around the world, but it was this chaplain who captured my full attention. Conversations with this gentleman launched my ten-year journey to find both the reason and the solution for man's problems. Neither of us knew at the time that through this encounter, God was also revealing His providential purpose for my life.

Having escaped from the Rwandan Conflict, the chaplain had traveled to the United States in order to make the people in our country, especially in church communities, aware of the carnage that was taking place in his homeland. From April to June 1994, the Hutu had massacred over 300,000 Tutsi, using mostly clubs and machetes. As we talked, he shared pictures—very graphic pictures—of the butchery. One photo, in particular, showed the bodies of the dead victims lying strewn across a churchyard. The images were heartbreaking, but it was the fact that these were Christians killing Christians that consumed me.

Determined to help deliver this message, I offered to take the chaplain to some churches in our area so that he could share what was happening in Rwanda. To my dismay, the church members responded with apathy. They then excused their indifference by asking, "Why should we get involved in the lives of people so far away?" These Christians were willing to dismiss the crisis in Rwanda, just as the world had abandoned the country when the United Nations Security Council voted unanimously to remove peacekeeping troops and leave the Tutsi and Hutu moderates behind. Without objection from other nations, the Hutu shifted into "genocidal mania"— clubbing and hacking to death defenseless Tutsi families. A Hutu soldier admitted, "It was as if we were taken over by Satan himself. When Satan is using you, you lose your mind.... You could not be normal and start butchering people for no reason."[1] Despite the enormity of the carnage, no one appeared to object.

Does Anyone Really Care?

While I struggled with the Christian response here, Paul Williams, M.D., author of the book *When All Plans Fail*, was encountering a disturbing lack of unity instead of what could have been a magnificent gesture to aid

the injured in the Hutu refugee camps in Zaire.
Dr. Williams offers this first-hand account:

> The day we landed in Goma, we were
> informed that thousands of people had
> already died from cholera, dysentery,
> meningitis, and malaria. Ten thousand
> bodies lined the dusty roads as we drove
> at a snail's pace to the refugee camp where
> we would set up our medical clinic. Psalm
> 91 was literally being fulfilled before my
> eyes. *"A thousand may fall at your side, and
> ten thousand at your right hand; but it shall
> not come near you. Only with your eyes shall
> you look, and see the reward of the wicked."*
> Having been in over 100 countries and
> worked in medical missions full time
> since 1984, I had observed much human
> suffering and need, but nothing like
> this. I'll never forget the empty gaze of
> children sitting beside their dead parents,
> or vice versa. I found myself crying as we
> drove along, witnessing the unspeakable
> scenes.[2]

I pondered this for a long time. Just as
I could "see" the innocent old woman who had

died at the hands of a drug-crazed addict, I could now see, through Dr. Paul's narrative, the innocent people—men, women, and children—who had died in the crossfire of a tribal war.

Why Are We Killing Each Other?

In the months that followed the conference, I could not stop watching the news as the conflict escalated. Three hundred thousand dead, the count rising. My heart was burdened, and my mind could not grasp this level of depravity. Six hundred thousand! It didn't stop...nine hundred thousand! Many of these people were friends and neighbors who had turned against each other. Something was terribly wrong.

Why, God? Why? Why are You letting all these innocent people die?

Suddenly I realized that this is nothing new—neighbors killing neighbors, even brothers killing brothers. It has been an all-too-familiar occurrence, repeated throughout history: for example, Northern Ireland, where Protestant Christians and Catholic Christians have been killing each other for generations. Or Bosnia, where Bosnian Serbs (Orthodox Catholic Christians) and Bosnian Muslims (Sunni), linguistically similar and close in bloodline, are killing each other. And, of course, there was the Civil War in the United States, where uncles killed nephews, fathers killed sons, and brothers killed brothers. All similarities, including kinships, between warring factions were simply ignored, and the inhumanity raged out of control. More recently, I have observed Iraq, where the Sunni branch of Islam and the Shiite branch of Islam have been killing each other.

The killing continues while those who could end it refuse to be their brother's keeper. Instead, they have chosen to be their brother's killer.

Fraternity or...Fratricide?

I began to see that we are caught in a *fratricidal deception* (*frat*—as in "fraternity or brotherhood"; *cide*, as in "suicide, homicide, and genocide—to kill"). *Fratricide* is the perfect term to describe this depraved state where brother kills brother, but why does mankind do this? Each "reason" I could find for fratricide revealed a level of deception that had actually led to a deeper level of depravity. This understanding produced a baffling dilemma.

As a Christian, I asked myself, *Did God create us to treat each other with such contempt?* The answer was obvious. *If not, then what is the reality at the basis of attempted genocides and fratricides such as these (and so many others)?* Thirty-one million killed in the Cultural Revolution in China, twenty million in the Great Leap Forward in China, twenty million in the Great Purge in the Soviet Union...

I needed to understand the truth about why brothers are killing brothers. What was the deception lurking beneath man's attempts to justify such horrific acts? My journey continued.

Enemy of God

The prisoner on Death Row was staring out the window at the street beyond. Restless and obviously agitated, he was bouncing on his toes, holding onto the bars. He turned around, looking right through me as if I were not even there.

I wanted to help him understand what had brought him to this point in life where he had been sentenced to death. "What made you stab her so many times?" I asked.

"Because she just wouldn't die."

"Do you know why you did that to your neighbor?"

"I knew it was wrong. I just needed the money."

"When everything was said and done, did it get you what you wanted?"

"Uh...no."

"Right! You wanted the good life, but you got the death sentence." I flipped open the Scriptures to the Book of James and began to read: *"Where do wars and fights come from among you? Do they not come from your desire for pleasure that war in your members? You lust and do not have. You murder and covet and cannot obtain. You fight and war and yet you do not have because you do not ask. You ask and do not receive because you ask amiss that you may spend it on your pleasures. Adulterers and adulteresses! Do you not know that friendship with the world is enmity with God? Whoever therefore wants to be a friend of the world makes himself an enemy of God"* (1:1-2).

He looked at me with a solemn gaze. "Man, why didn't I know this? Think I could have stopped it?"

"Yes, son, I do."

"How?"

"By knowing the truth."

"What's the truth?"

"Let me break it down for you."

What Is the Truth?

That day I began spelling out truth for a condemned killer. But the answer applies to every one of us. Beneath the layers of "reasons"—justifiable excuses—given to explain the atrocities that man commits against man, there must be a singular truth to explain *the* reality at the basis of the issues in life. In Scripture, the word *truth* comes from the Greek word *aletheia*, meaning *"the* reality at the basis of an *appearance*," or "the *manifested, veritable* essence of a matter."[3]

Appearance—"outwardly superficial, transitory or changeable, as opposed to what is eternal and essential."

Manifested—"immediately evident to the senses, mind and perception."

Veritable—"real or actual, having all the qualities or attributes of the specified person or thing."[4]

Truth, therefore, reveals the reality that is at the basis of what is outwardly superficial, transitory or changeable.

Let's take a closer look at the three key words in the definition of truth: appearance, manifest, and veritable.

Appearance (outward, superficial and changeable) is demonstrated nearly every day of our lives. When we look into a mirror, we see what is outward, superficial, and changeable, as opposed to that part of us that is unseen, eternal and essential (the soul). This is what we experience in the world, in our societies. This outward, superficial, transitory, changeable façade is like the shell of a sea animal or the cocoon from which a butterfly emerges. Clearly, the shell and the cocoon are not the true essence of these little creatures. When we, by chance, are afforded a glimpse beyond the facade, we ask, "What is the truth? What is the reality at the basis of this appearance? What is eternal? What IS the soul?"

Manifest (immediately evident to the senses, mind, and perception) seemed a contradiction in that I could not trust my senses beyond their perception of the appearance. To accurately discern truth, I had to turn to the source of Truth, the inerrant, infallible Word of God—the "Book." It was only when I went to the source of Truth that I was able to clearly understand the issues of life.

When I share truth from the Holy Scriptures, people light up and say, "Ahhh." Connections are made and reality is revealed.

They conclude: "There is something to this." That is what truth does. It reveals; a light comes on. That's what the apostle John meant when he said, *"In Him was life, and the life was the light of men"* (1:4) He was describing Jesus who came into the world to shed light on our situation by bringing insight as to what the problem with us really is. When we experience truth from the Holy Scriptures, it brings into light what was hidden in darkness; it makes truth immediately evident to our senses, our minds, and our perceptions.

Veritable (real or actual—unchanging) must include all of the qualities of a specific person or thing—qualities both seen and unseen. Only through the study of Scripture could I fully understand the final key word. Without one, unchanging truth, all of life's issues, including the Rwandan Conflict, seemed volatile and confusing. When I began to deal with life according to the truth, I understood that I did not have to *physically* see all the qualities or attributes of something. The Holy Scriptures repeatedly state that mankind has a *spiritual* element to his being.

I was dealing with human beings, yet I was dealing with life beyond the attributes and qualities immediately evident to my senses.

Therefore, when we hear and accept all that is real, actual, and unchanging from the Holy Scriptures, the reality at the basis of what is outwardly superficial, transitory, or changeable becomes immediately evident. Then we bring it into our practical everyday lives and it becomes real and actual. We begin to know and experience the truth.

The Quest for Truth

Now that I had a definition for Truth, where was I to find it? As a believer, I was taught to go to the Holy Scriptures, but I cannot limit truth to my experience only. Each person, community, or culture cannot have its own truth; by definition, truth is *the* reality at the basis of an appearance—*the*, meaning "specific," allowing for only one truth.

If there is only one truth, the Holy Books should agree. I began researching three of them—the Quran, the Old Testament, and the New Testament.

What Does the Quran Say about Truth?

The Quran, "the recitation," is the Muslim Holy Book, which Islamic peoples believe to be the book of divine guidance and direction for mankind, revealed to Muhammad. The book itself is divided into 114 chapters, called suras, dealing more with moral issues than with the historical record of a people.[5]

> Sura 10:94:
>
> *If you have any doubt regarding what is revealed to you from your Lord, then ask those who read the previous scriptures, indeed, the truth has come to you from your Lord. Do not be with the doubters.*

Muslims who do not understand or those who have questions are told to "go to the people of the Book." When I looked in the Quran and researched references on that verse, the "people of the Book" were those who study the Holy Scriptures, the inerrant, infallible Word of God, which was inspired by His Spirit and recorded by a large number of men over a long span of years. It was given *"for doctrine, for reproof, for correction, for instruction in righteousness"* (2 Timothy 3:16).

What Does the Old Testament Say about Truth?

The Old Testament, the first major division of the Christian Holy Bible, consists of thirty-nine chapters, dealing with the Law (the five books of Moses), history of the Hebrew people, poetical books (Job-Song of Solomon), and prophetical books (Isaiah-Malachi).[6]

Hebrew Psalm 119:89:
Forever, O LORD, thy word is settled in heaven.

Hebrew Psalm 119:160:
Thy Word is true from the beginning: and every one of thy righteous judgments endures forever.

These verses are from the people to

whom God gave the original Scriptures, the people referred to in the Quran.

What Does the New Testament Say about Truth?

The New Testament, the second major division of the Christian Bible, or New Covenant, consists of four narratives of the life and ministry of Jesus Christ ("Gospels"), a narrative of the Apostles' ministries in the early church, twenty-one letters ("epistles"), and an Apocalyptic prophecy ("Revelation).[7]

John 1:14:

> *And the Word became flesh and dwelt among us, and we beheld His glory, the glory as of the only begotten of the Father, full of grace and truth* [the realities at the basis of the issues of life.]

John 14:6:

> *Jesus said to him, "I am the Way, the Truth, and the Life. No one comes to the Father except through Me."*

So where was I to look for truth? Muslims say, "Go to the Holy Scriptures." Jews say, "Go to the Holy Scriptures." Christians say, "Go to the Holy Scriptures." So if I am to know the realities at the basis of the appearance, I must go to the Book that reveals the truth to me. If Muslims, Jews, and Christians all agree on the Holy Scriptures as the source for truth, I should start there and not with the documents of the secularists.

Georgina Dufoix, former French Minister of Family Affairs, recently stated, "In Europe, people are at a point where many are acknowledging that humanism does not have the answers to their problems."[8] Why is it that we want our issues to default to psychology, sociology, philosophy, or politics when it is increasingly clear that these disciplines really don't have any of the answers? Why are we failing to get at the root of the problem?

Revealed truth causes us to default to Creation and the Creator for our answers. When I began to search the Scriptures for the truth about man's inhumanity to man, I learned that God created a pattern for dealing with conflict before the foundations of the world.[10] We need to re-connect with our Creator to determine how life is to be lived. He's the only One who knows. It is His pattern we must discover.

Before that, however, we need to go back and find the fatal flaw that brought about our dilemma, or we'll *never* come up with the solution to our problems.

THERE'S A CURIOUS CONSISTENCY TO THE ISSUES THAT CAUSE CONFLICT, VIOLENCE AND CONFRONTATION ACROSS EVERY CONTINENT. WHEN I DISCOVER THE REALITY AT THE BASIS OF MY ISSUES, I ALSO DISCOVER THE SAME IN ALL OTHERS. MY ISSUES IN MY CULTURE ARE NOT UNIQUE.

2

DECEPTION:
THE TRUTH
ABOUT BEING DECEIVED

SATAN'S FAVORITE TOOL FOR CREATING CONFLICT

"And He said,
'Who told you that you were naked?
Have you eaten from the tree
of which I commanded you
that you should not eat?'
"Then the man said,
'The woman whom you gave to be with me,
she gave me of the tree, and I ate.'
"And the Lord God said to the woman,
'What is this you have done?'
The woman said,
'The serpent deceived me, and I ate.'"

GENESIS 3:11-13

When I was a young believer, an older gentleman said, "Son, if you ever want to know
why the world is the way it is—why people do
the things they do—go to the book of beginning. Go to the Book of Genesis." Following
his advice, I spent five years studying the first
book of the Holy Scriptures.

My need to understand why the Hutu
and the Tutsi massacred each other was the
beginning of my discovery of the deception
that lies hidden beneath man's "reasons" for
his wrongful behavior. To uncover more about
deception, I started with the definition, then
began to study the term in the Scriptures.

Deception gives a false impression,
whether by appearance, statement, or
influence; it makes a person believe as true
something that is false; it misleads or tends

to lead into error. The key word, *false*, means "devoid of truth, containing error, containing fundamental errors in reasoning, not true to duty or obligation, and fraudulently or deceptively imitative."

Truth, by sheer opposition, must reveal deception, so if man has had truth available throughout time, why has the world taken the path so plagued with deception? Continuing to read the news coming out of Rwanda, I still wanted to know how people could be deceived into believing the inconsistencies offered as justification for the carnage—so many conflicting "truths."

Back to the Beginning

In Genesis, we have the record of creation. We read that God created the world, He created man, He created the Garden of Eden, and He saw that everything was good. God placed Adam in the Garden to tend it and commanded him, *"Of every tree of the garden you may freely eat; but of the tree of the knowledge of good and evil, you shall not eat."* And then that divine judgment, *"For in the day that you eat of it you shall surely die"* (Genesis 2:16-17).

God knew that it was not good for man to be alone, so He put Adam to sleep, took a rib from his side, and made woman.

As the story continues, Adam and Eve were in the Garden together when the serpent tempted Eve to eat the fruit of the forbidden tree and caused her to doubt God. *"Has God indeed said, 'You shall not eat of every tree of the garden?'"* (Genesis 3:1). She listened. She pondered his question. And in entertaining the serpent's subtle suggestion—that God really didn't mean what He said—she gave way to rationalization and picked the fruit. Finding it delicious to the taste, she offered it to Adam, and he ate. Eve was deceived; Adam was disobedient. Was that the truth I was searching for?

If so, it was the most unfair thing I had ever heard! Thus began a season of questioning and debating God.

Conversations with the Creator

"I didn't do anything, Lord, so why are

You penalizing me for something Adam did?" It all seemed grossly unfair!

Adam ate from the tree...so what? What's the big deal? What's so mystical about the Tree of the Knowledge of Good and Evil? Why did God create such a tree if He didn't want man to eat from it? Why was Adam so weak? I had to get hold of Adam's disobedience from God's perspective. I needed to know the truth behind Adam's actions if I were ever going to understand how his sin had made it necessary for God to provide a means to reconcile us to Himself.

We Were Created to Choose

First, God helped me see that man's free will was pointless if there were no choice involved. Adam had a clear choice—to eat or not to eat. I sensed God saying in my spirit, *"Adam not only chose to disobey Me, but he shifted the blame—first to Me, then to Eve—and did not accept responsibility for his own actions. Adam justified his disobedience in his own mind."*

Even after Adam sinned, God still chose

relationship. Walking in the Garden in the cool of the day, he called, *"Adam, where are you?"* From his hiding place among the trees, Adam replied, *"I was naked, and I hid myself."* God then asked, *"Who told you that you were naked? Have you eaten from the tree?"* To this, Adam answered, *"The woman, that you gave me, gave me the fruit and I did eat"* (Genesis 3:8-12).

Once I understood the need for man's ability to exercise this God-given free will, I could stop blaming Him for man's fall and start looking at truth in a new light.

Keeping God at a Distance

Sin, by definition, is going contrary to God's plan. It is willful disobedience; it is missing the mark; it is deviating from God's will. God is omniscient (all-knowing), omnipresent (in all places), and omnipotent (all-powerful). He is the Sovereign Creator, and Adam disobeyed Him. What I learned was that sin does not keep man separated from God. Knowing that His creation would sin, God had already planned the means of atonement before He created man. It is man's continued iniquity that keeps God "at a distance."

It took me five years to see the truth of what Adam had done; his action went far beyond sinning. *By doing what he wanted to do, when he wanted to do it, the way he wanted to do it,* without accepting responsibility for his actions, he was guilty of one of man's most troubling problems—iniquity.

While reading Job 31, I found an upright Old Testament man struggling with this very thing. As I meditated on Job's words, my own thoughts surfaced:

> *I have made a covenant with my eyes; Why then should I look upon a young woman? For what is the allotment of God from above, and the inheritance of the Almighty from on high? Is it not destruction for the wicked, and disaster for the workers of iniquity? Does He not see my ways, and count all my steps (vv. 1-4)?*

As a young man and now, in the winter of my years, God has revealed to me that He is aware of everything in my life. That one fact keeps me humble before Him, repentant toward Him, and dependent upon Him because I know that, in my own power, I cannot avoid the multitude of "urges" that prod me daily to stray from His path. My eyes, my feet, my hands, and my ears can, on any given day, lead me to violate His will for my life. I can, thus, clearly identify with the role that temptation played upon Adam and Eve in the Garden. Alone, I am helpless before it.

> *If I have walked with falsehood, or if my foot has hastened to deceit, let me be weighed on honest scales, that God may know my integrity (vv. 5-6).*

In nearly all of my dealings with people, I find virtues like honesty and integrity either ignored or forgotten. Deceit is so pervasive that I now understand just how unavoidable it is. Without God's help, my own fall, like Adam's, is equally unavoidable. I can now see why sin and iniquity demand justice. Adam and Eve were weighed on God's scales of justice and were obviously found lacking. Jesus Christ is the only choice I can make in my otherwise feeble attempts to balance those scales.

If I have kept the poor from their desire, or caused the eyes of the widow to fail, or eaten my morsel by myself, so that the fatherless could not eat of it….

…If I have seen anyone perish for lack of clothing, or any poor man without covering… if I have raised my hand against the fatherless, when I saw I had help in the gate; then let my arm fall from my shoulder, let my arm be torn from the socket (vv. 16-22).

In all of my travels throughout the world, I have seen poverty, helplessness, and hopelessness that surpass anything I could ever have imagined. Sadly, I have also witnessed a matching level of apathy toward those conditions and their multitude of victims. I have had to ask myself, "Who am I *not* to attempt to do something to help alleviate all this suffering?" I can no more turn my back on those who suffer than I can fail to take my next breath.

If I have made gold my hope, or said to fine gold, 'You are my confidence'; If I have rejoiced because my wealth was great, and because my hand had gained much;...

This also would be an iniquity deserving of judgment, for I would have denied God who is above (vv. 24, 28).

I was once among those obsessed with the pursuit of material gain, knowing all the while that Solomon himself, the richest man of all time, likened that quest to "chasing after the wind." It never occurred to me until recently that the truly richest man on earth was Adam. If there ever was one who "had it all," it was he. I can only shake my head when I think what he lost—what all of us lost. But I am encouraged by God's promise of so much more...

If I have rejoiced at the destruction of him who hated me, or lifted myself up when evil found him... If I have covered my transgressions as Adam, by hiding my iniquity in my bosom...(vv. 29, 33).

I suppose it is natural to feel anger toward those who persecute the helpless or wrong others in any way, but life has taught me that, in my anger, I am saying, "I am better than such people....." My thought is stopped short by the realization that it is this very attitude that is at the core of all conflicts. To this day, I continue to fail; I continue to "fall short." I see myself in Adam. This, I think, is what Job ultimately came to realize. This, I think, is that special, divine gift—the awareness that the years bring to the minds of the truly wise.

The birth of iniquity was the beginning of man's choice to misplace blame, justify sin, and avoid responsibility. In Adam, man began exercising his God-given free will to act contrary to God's will without accepting blame. Iniquity has plagued man ever since. This single incident in history has resulted in all kinds of complexities in life—all levels of conflict. Sin is the wrongful act, and iniquity is the attempt to justify it. *Excuses lead to refusals to reconcile and align with God's will. Adam disobeyed God, stepped off His path, and created an alternative path for man to follow.*

I then realized that like Adam, I too have the choice to say no to God. It is evident to me now that my choices have often been offensive to God. I also know that continuing on that path ultimately leads to self-destruction.

Adam's actions made it necessary for us to be reconciled to God in order to know God's plan and purpose for life, to return to the truth, and to walk within God's perfect will— loving our brother as He originally intended. I could be forgiven for my sins, but it is only on God's path that I can become my brother's keeper instead of my brother's killer.

"Unrepented" Iniquity Leads to Death

The iniquitous nature of mankind was passed down from Adam and Eve to the next generation. Both Cain and Abel, two of Adam's sons, knew what was required of them by God when it came to "appropriate" sacrifices, yet each took a separate path—one that God had demonstrated; the other, man's choice.

In Genesis, after Adam and Eve chose to exercise their will in the Garden, God "made garments of (animal) skin" to cover their nakedness. In so doing, He was establishing forever the means of atonement between Himself and man—the shedding of blood—so that sin would not create an eternal separation between them. For *"where there is no shedding of blood, there is no remission of sin"* (Hebrews 9:22).[1] We associate blood with death and gore, but God associates blood with life (see Leviticus 17:11). He is dealing with us through the source of life.

When Cain and Abel presented their sacrifices to God, Abel followed God's model and offered the firstborn of his flock—an acceptable offering. Cain, on the other hand, chose to ignore God's plan and brought a sacrifice from his harvest, a sacrifice that lacked the necessary blood. God rejected it.

Cain was extremely upset. *"Why are you angry?"* God asked him. *"And why has your countenance fallen? If you do well, will you not be accepted? And if you do not do well, sin lies at the door. And its desire is for you, but you should rule over it"* (Genesis 4:6-7). In other words, God was telling him, "Your problem is with Me, not with your brother. You need to follow the set rules for atonement and reconcile with Me. Choose My path, not yours."

But what did Cain do? He refused

instruction from the Creator of life. Not only did he fail to hear and obey God's clear command, but he attacked and killed his brother! At that moment, when Cain chose to turn his back on his Creator, iniquity began to run its rampant course in the earth.

The End of Innocence

Cain had no problem with his brother; it was not Abel who rejected his offering. It was God Himself who rejected it.

At this point, I learned that more than murder had taken place in that incident. Worldly innocence had been destroyed. Abel, as simple and trusting as a child, was a grown man; yet he was innocent, free from guile. With his death, that pure state of existence was also destroyed.[2] Abel had followed God's established rules for atonement, and though he had done nothing wrong, his life was taken. Again it seemed unfair. Abel did what he was told, yet he was murdered.

Throughout those five years of studying Genesis, I tried to figure out what had instigated the world's first murder. I wondered what Cain and Abel talked about when they were together. Nowhere in Scripture does it ever say. Never is it mentioned what Abel might have said or done that would cause Cain to kill him. I thought that surely Abel must have said something to provoke his brother, but nothing at all is recorded. This must have been intentional. God wants us to know that Abel was innocent.

I'll never forget the early months of my baseball career. Some folks called me naïve, but I was really just young and innocent—so wet behind the ears that geese could land! When I left home for Chandler, Arizona—three thousand miles from home—I was wearing a three-piece suit. When I got off the bus, the other guys on the team were all decked out in jeans, cowboy boots and hats. What did I know? That was back in 1962, when the threat of war with Russia had the older guys worrying about the draft. At seventeen, I was too young to register! !

Looking back now, I can see that God had my back. He put several of my teammates in place to look out for me. One of them was Hal Wade, a college graduate at the time, now president of a college in Atlanta. In one game I was pitching, he was the catcher. I remember his cautioning me, "I want you to throw everything I tell you tonight and don't shake me off." Daddy and Ma had taught me well. I obeyed...and was rewarded with a two-hitter game!

Like Abel, I followed the rules and gave my best, but I soon found that people can take advantage of you if you aren't wise to their ways. While playing for the Pittsburgh organization, I was drafted by the Boston Red Sox. The contract they sent by mail called for a salary of only a little more than I was making with the Pirates. I still didn't know much, but I knew that didn't sound right, so I called a friend, a scout from the Pittsburgh Pirates.

When I told him my problem, he came over to talk with me. "That figure doesn't sound right to me either, Jack—not for a Major League contract. Do you have another phone in the house?"

I got on the line in another room while he dialed a contact he had, also by the name of Harry. When Harry Postove answered, Harry Land said, "I have a young man here who just got drafted by the Red Sox. But they're only offering him $450 a month."

What I heard next jolted me. "Is the kid black?" he asked, not knowing I was listening in.

"Wh-what difference does that make?" Harry Land sputtered.

"Well, you know how it is," the other Harry went on. "They try to get those guys as cheap as possible."

I grew up that day. I saw the truth— the reality at the basis of the appearance, the manifest, veritable essence of the matter! I guess I could have hated that guy. I tried to hate him, but I never did.

Again I questioned God, "How could you let this happen? Why does the innocent man suffer as a result of the iniquity of the sinful man?" I was still trying to understand these issues without a complete grasp of the truth. I was looking at it, however, from an earthly point of view—the same point of view that is the prime motivator behind the many "social issues" that continue to destroy innocence today.

God's Answer

God finally revealed more of the truth to me. I realized that Abel, after his death, remained in good standing with God. Despite Abel's murder, he was not punished (spiritually speaking). There is quite a difference. That punishment would have involved separation from God. Hebrews 11:4 reveals the truth about Abel: *"By faith, Abel offered God a better sacrifice than Cain. By faith, he was commended as a righteous man when God spoke well of his offerings, and by faith, he still speaks, even though he is dead."* In Genesis 4:10, God asked Cain, *"What have you done? The voice of your brother's blood cries out to Me from the ground."*[2] These passages prove that Abel never lost his relationship with God.

From this, I learned that I had to stop trying to judge God as being unfair, not only because He is sovereign, but also because I do not have the full understanding of His purpose, motive, and objective in every situation. What I saw as punishment lacked the scriptural meaning—separation from God.

Dealing with Life Man to Man

With Adam, the whole world became guilty of sin before God. As a result, iniquity was born. With Cain, iniquity and deception combined to create the ultimate lie—that we can deal with life's conflicts and confrontations man to man. The deception at the root of these difficult issues lies in man's attempts to resolve them through other humans like ourselves when they are really man-to-God issues. We can truly reconcile with each other only after we reconcile with God.

I must emphasize that we have to go to the One who created life in order to understand how life is to be lived. The Creator has a plan to guide His creation. For true reconciliation to take place, God's plan requires the victim to initiate reconciliation through forgiveness, freeing the perpetrator to repent and to demonstrate remorse. (See Appendix A.)

Man did not create life; therefore, he cannot create a real purpose or a plan for life. His only purpose or plan is limited by human viewpoint, ability, power, and life span on earth. Man's plans, in the absence of God's will, end up being iniquitous and inevitably take man down the path that ultimately leads to self-destruction.

Deception Revealed

As I reviewed my research on the Rwandan massacres, I saw how these Christians had left God out of their lives and had taken matters into their own hands. This mindset led to murder. I studied the reported sequence of historical "facts," hoping to find the deceptions. I found the "fact" that hatred had developed between the Hutu and the Tutsi as a result of a division that grew out of colonialism. Reports explained how European colonizers pitted the Hutu and the Tutsi against each other by giving the Tutsi basic ruling rights over the Hutu. These colonizers conducted "scientific" studies and claimed that the Tutsi were "racially superior." Simultaneously, they took away all ruling class positions and authority from the so-called "inferior" Hutu. A deceptive racial divide was created, and racial identification cards were issued. Even though the Hutu and Tutsi occupied the same geographic areas, spoke the same languages, and shared a common history, they fell victim to the subtle yet very tragic deception.

As I studied more, I learned that prejudice had existed centuries before, when the Tutsi came from the North and established a feudalist regime over the Hutu majority. The divide was based upon cattle, not land ownership. In most basic terms, the Tutsi were cattlemen and the Hutu were farmers. I had finally found a difference between the warring factions, and though it did not seem enough to foster murder, it was an answer.

Then deception was again revealed. In an article I learned that the Tutsi and the Hutu were not in fixed social classes.[3] Phil Clark explained that the categories were "permeable." A Hutu who gained sufficient wealth, usually in the form of cattle, could become a Tutsi. Likewise, a Tutsi who lost his wealth could become Hutu.[4] Again, the reasons turned out to be deceptions—man-made excuses to justify sinful behavior and, ultimately, iniquity.

Deception with Iniquity
Leads to Depravity

Now I began to understand. I could see past the deception that was hidden beneath "reasons" for the bloody massacre between the Hutu and the Tutsi. Deception played a part, but iniquity played the key role. The warring factions were deceived, believing, yet again, that they could deal with life's issues man-to-man instead of man-to-God. This left no opportunity for true reconciliation to take place.

The deception was in thought, but iniquity "materialized" as sin in the form of fratricide. Choices were made; man's path was chosen; machetes were swung and thousands died. Man's choices, again, led to death. His rules were not aligned with God's purpose, God's plan, and God's objective.

Without God, the deception becomes so complete that truth is obscured and man becomes depraved—blinded to God's will and purpose. Intellectually it made sense. But my heart broke when God met me in that place of pain where I continued to wrestle with the question: *"Why are You letting the innocent suffer and die?"*

The answer came deep in my spirit, in that familiar, still, small voice. *"They are not just at war with each other. They are killing Me!"*

I buried my head in my hands, and I wept....

TRUTH REVEALS THE DECEPTION THAT HAS CAUSED US TO BELIEVE THAT OUR CONFLICT IS WITH OUR BROTHER AND NOT WITH GOD.

3

DEPRAVITY:
THE ULTIMATE EFFECT
OF
SIN AND INIQUITY

WHAT HAPPENS WHEN WE HAVE OUR OWN WAY

"They exchanged the truth of God for a lie, and worshiped and served the creature rather than the Creator…and just as they did not see fit to acknowledge God any longer, God gave them over to a depraved mind, to do those things which are not proper."

ROMANS 1:25, 28 NASB

What my chaplain friend saw and photographed in Rwanda—those graphic images of man's inhumanity to man—have lived in my memory ever since. No matter what I do, I cannot dismiss them as inconsequential. They still speak to me of what happens when we follow a path other than God's intended path for the human race. Continued and habitual sin, justifying the sin and refusing to take personal responsibility for it eventually leads to utter disregard for God's laws or even for His feelings.

After a while, one's spiritual nerve endings become less and less sensitive, maybe even die, and the human mind takes over as creator. Utterly deceived, man thinks he can create his own rules. Since God does not retract His gifts, the human mind, capable of great creativity, concocts increasingly evil plans. Unrestrained by the Holy Spirit, these plans and intents of the heart may result in horrific actions, such as those that took place in Rwanda. This state of mind and being is known as depravity.

Dead Men Walking

It is possible, even while one is still alive, to be dead (see 1Timothy 5:6). In fact, because of the Fall and until we are awakened by the Spirit of the Living God, we are born spiritually "dead." But when, after becoming old enough to hear His voice, one chooses to disregard His call and walk in defiance and rebellion, that person will likely descend to ever lower levels of sin. Depravity is the condition of being utterly reprehensible in nature or behavior; it includes immoral, degrading acts or habits; it is willful separation from God.

In order to gain the fullest under-standing of depravity, I looked up all the synonyms for this word. Like my friend's photograph album, one horrifying "picture" followed another: "corrupt, immoral, base, debased, debauched, degenerate, degraded, dirty, dirty-minded, dissolute, evil, filthy, lascivious, lewd, licentious, low, mean, nefarious, perverted, putrid, rotten, shameless, sinful, twisted, unhealthy, unnatural, vicious, vile, villainous, wanton, warped, wicked."[1] The longer man tries to live without God's presence, the more commonplace demented behavior becomes.

Now we see that the reality at the basis of the appearance of the issues in this life lay in Adam's disobedience, which opened an iniquitous path. That path has matured into the otherwise inexplicable state of depravity we see everywhere today.

Depraved minds cause people to commit atrocities such as those in Rwanda, Northern Ireland, and Iraq. When man steps away from God, truth is perverted, and we begin to see alternative "truths"; deceptive practices become common and are even accepted as "normal." Good and evil often appear on the same stage, causing confusion, conflict and chaos.

Murder and Mayhem

In researching what man has done to others, I found some of the worst massacres in all of human history. These are listed from the largest number of people slaughtered to the smallest, not by date of occurrence:[2]

- 40,000,000 Chinese   1850-1864
  Chinese Taiping Rebellion
- 40,000,000 Chinese   1210-1240
  Mongols--conquest of North China
- 15,000,000 Russians   1941-1945
  Nazi Germany (Civilians) Conquest
- 12,000,000 Jews   1933-1945
  Jewish Holocaust, Nazi Germany
- 12,000,000 Africans   1400-1880
  Atlantic Slave-trade
- 5,000,000 Asians   1370-1405
  Timurlane Wars
- 5,000,000 Japanese   1945-1950
  Chinese, Russians Maltreatment Camps
- 5,000,000 Vietnamese   1954-1965
  Hanoi Red Terror Purge Labor Camps
- 5,000,000 Sudanese   1960-1987
  Sudanese Civil War

- 2,000,000 Hindu   N/A -1850
  Religious Custom: "Suttee"
- 2,000,000 Indians   1500-1850
  Thugee Cult-Ritual Caste Murder
- 1,500,000 Cambodians   1975-1978
  Red Terror Khmer Rouge Regime
- 1,000,000 Armenians   1916-1918
  Turks, Kurds Genocide
- 1,000,000 Nigerians   1966-1969
  Nigeria The "Biafran War"
- 1,000,000 Indonesians   1942-1945
  Japan's Maltreatment of Labor Camps
- 1,000,000 Japanese   1943-1945
  American Terror Bombing
- 500,000 Americans   1861-1865
  United States Civil War

This is a "snapshot" of what is wrong with our society. The numbers and dates are somewhat misleading. Even though it appears that mankind may have "improved" over the course of time and there are fewer incidents of global genocide today, the fact that human beings still attempt to wipe out whole tribes or races is testimony to their depravity. The only difference is that current attempts to obliterate masses of people lie in the subtlety with which the attacks are made. Consider abortion, for example...fifty million innocent little babies aborted since 1973!

How can human beings stoop to such barbaric acts? How can their consciences allow it?

General Romeo Dallaire, a U.N. officer in Rwanda during the genocide, tells of his experiences in an interview with some Rwandan militants. The interview was conducted in the partially bombed-out Diplomat Hotel in Kigali, where General Dallaire was introduced to the three Rwandans. As they shook hands, the general noticed that their clothing was spattered with blood.

"All of a sudden, something happened that turned them into non-humans," he reports. "I was not talking with humans. I literally was talking with evil personified... maybe in those bodies and with those eyes... but they weren't human. And what was coming out of their mouths was not human. What was coming out was not the words of a human negotiating or discussing; it was evil, blurting out positions and arguments. I didn't see human beings anymore. I was totally overcome by the evil...."[3]

Taking innocent life by brutal means is the result of a seared conscience, one that is no longer in touch with the Creator of life.

Man's Primary Enemy— From Genesis to Jesus

In my workshops, I often ask, "Who is the primary enemy of man?" Seventy-five percent of the people respond, "Satan." Twenty-four percent say, "Man." Only 1 percent understand that Scripture clearly reveals that God is man's primary enemy.[4]

Man is not naturally kind, not naturally considerate, not naturally good—just the opposite of God. People rarely think about it, but a baby does not have to be taught to be selfish or aggressive, but must be taught (consistently and sometimes forcefully) all the "nice skills," like sharing and patience.

We live in contrast to innocence; we are domineering and power-seeking. In our iniquity, we want to create our own reality, which is contrary to God's will. In other words, we have ignored God's purpose, motive, and objective for our creation by exercising our (God-given) free will to do so. Thus, we suffer the consequences that result from doing things our way.

At war with God, man becomes utterly reprehensible and immoral; he performs degrading acts and takes on shameful habits. He ignores God's will and creates his own rules to satisfy often sordid temptations that spiral downward.

Tasting Forbidden Fruit

One of the greatest examples of succumbing to temptation is the biblical story of David, king of Israel. While one of his generals was off in battle, David saw the young general's wife, Bathsheba, bathing on a rooftop. David was impressed and sent for her. You know what happened next. It is recorded for all time in God's Word (see 2 Samuel 11:1-17)[5], perhaps as a means of warning all of us whose natural instincts are to do what we want to do when we want to do it!

If your story were written down for all the world to read, would it sound like David's story? Together, idle time and the seductive beauty of a young woman resulted in an irresistible temptation for David. Bathsheba became pregnant. In an attempt to cover his sin, he sent for her husband and suggested that Uriah spend the night with his wife.

Unwilling to experience the pleasures of life while his men were on the battlefield, the honorable general refused. Frustrated, David sent him to the front where the fighting was most fierce. General Uriah was killed soon afterward. Doing what David wanted to do, when he wanted to do it, the way he wanted to do it ultimately led to another grievous sin--- the murder of one of his most trusted men.

Even then, in the face of this grave offense against God, David did not turn to Him immediately, but continued on his iniquitous path. Sin breeds more sin. Repeated and unforgiven sin gives birth to iniquity.

It was some time later that God sent the prophet Nathan to confront David with the truth. Unlike too many, David repented with great grief: *"God, against You, and You only have I committed this sin*" (Psalm 51:4).[6]

The Lord had rule over David, so it was the Lord whom David ultimately defied—not other men. So, he asked God to blot out his iniquity. This time, when God gave a choice for man (David) to reconcile, he stepped back onto God's path, thus following His will. Even though David had committed vile sins, he took responsibility for his iniquity and was willing to deal with life's issues man to God. He acknowledged God's sovereignty, accepted reconciliation, and was later identified by God as "*a man after His own heart*" (Acts 13: 22).[7]

In the New Testament, Jesus told His disciples, "*When you feed the hungry, when you visit the sick, when you visit those in prison… when you have done it to the least one of these, you have done it to me*" (see Matthew 25:31-45, author's paraphrase). Logically, we must understand that when we commit atrocities against one another, we have also committed these atrocities against God.

Until we grasp this concept, we will continue to kill our brothers one way or another, which leads to a perplexing dilemma.

Chalice of Depravity

*"And even as they did not like to retain God
in their knowledge, God gave them over to a
debased mind, to do those things which are not
fitting; being filled with all unrighteousness,
sexual immorality, wickedness, covetousness,
maliciousness; full of envy, murder,
strife, deceit, evil-mindedness;
they are whisperers,
backbiters,
haters of God,
violent,
proud,
boasters,
inventors of evil things,
disobedient to parents,
undiscerning,
untrustworthy,
unloving,
unforgiving,
unmerciful;
who, knowing the
righteous judgment of God,
that those who practice such things
are deserving of death, not only do the same
but also approve of those who practice them."*

Romans 1:28-32

DILEMMA:
LIFE...OR DEATH?

RECONCILIATION WITH GOD AND MAN
IS A CHOICE.

"I have set before you life and death,
blessing and cursing;
therefore choose life."

DEUTERONOMY 30:19

Recently I was invited to hear a speech given by a friend of mine at a gathering in Washington, D. C. That night I was delayed in traffic and arrived at the venue late. When I walked in, I slipped into the back, aware that I had missed my friend. But what I heard sent shivers down my spine. The crowd was passionate. They were yelling and screaming at the top of their lungs, "Reparations...or death! Reparations...or death!"

At the height of their hysteria, one of the attendees walked over. He was apparently curious about why I was not joining in. "What's the matter? Aren't you with us?"

In my mind, I was seeing the piles of dead bodies from the Rwandan genocide... men, women, and children, dismembered and mutilated...mothers wailing for their dead children…babies crying for their mothers…

If they only knew what they are starting here tonight… "What you need to know is the reality at the basis of the appearance," I said, feeling a deep sorrow within.

The man yelled at me again. "Wh-what? What are you talking about?"

Three hundred thousand…nine hundred thousand…how many deaths will it take to satisfy their thirst? I spoke more slowly this time. "I said that you really ought to understand…the reality…at the basis of the appearance…."

"Say that again!"

Does it really matter? Will they hear me…or will they just continue on their path of violence and bloodlust? He *had* to understand. I repeated myself for the third time.

Suddenly the young man lifted his head and stared at me, his eyes narrowing. His passion cooled, and grasping his dilemma, he turned and walked away.

A mindset that promotes "reparations" rather than biblical reconciliation can cause people to overlook the very signs that can lead to another Rwanda.

What Is the Dilemma?

Dilemma is defined as a choice between equally balanced alternatives; it is a predicament that defies satisfactory solution. Man's iniquitous path has led us into an unavoidable state of depravity which, in turn, places us in the middle of a life-or-death dilemma.

Paul captures this struggle in his words, *"The things I do, I don't want to do, but the things I don't do, I want to do....O wretched man, who would deliver me from the body of this death?"* (Romans 7:15, 24 NIV).[1] Like Paul, only when we know truth, are we able to identify the hidden iniquity in our actions against each other. Only when we have identified the facts about our nature is it possible to understand that, like Adam, our choice to sin is nothing less than blatant defiance of God—attempts to do things our way.

When we fall for the deception, believing we are smart enough to figure out all of life's issues ourselves—when we value our counsel above God's—we become His enemy by default. Again, we move down that path of iniquity that leads to a state of depravity that ultimately forces us into a situation where we must make a choice between equally balanced alternatives. Our predicament lies in the fact that, on the iniquitous path, there is no satisfactory solution. This is mankind's ultimate dilemma.

There is a struggle that inevitably takes place within us when we do not follow God's will. When we exercise our will, we place ourselves in a self-destructive paradigm that changes us from sinful to iniquitous to deceived to depraved. Once that state of depravity is reached, we become locked in a dilemma that defies resolution.

Who Is the Real Victim?

In 1999, I was part of a committee that put together a conference in Africa. The president of Benin wanted to make a public apology to all African-Americans (and all of the Africans of the Diaspora) for his ancestors having sold their ancestors into slavery. Representatives from the United States, Europe, and regional chiefs and kings came and participated in this Conference of Reconciliation.[2]

Andrew Young, former United States Ambassador to the United Nations and top aide to Dr. Martin Luther King during the civil rights movement, was solicited to make a statement of forgiveness on behalf of the African-American Diaspora. When he became ill, it was decided that I would make the statement of forgiveness. Feeling poorly equipped to handle this tremendous assignment, I went out into my backyard and began to pray.

"Lord," I began, "what do I say on behalf of the African-American Diaspora in making a statement of forgiveness for having been so victimized? What do I say as the victim?"

As I continued to walk and pray, I paused for a while. The voice wasn't necessarily audible, but this communication started taking place in my mind:

"I'm the victim," God answered me.

"What?"

Again I heard, *"I'm the victim."*

Yet a third time, the still, small voice said, *"I'm the victim."*

After the third time, God revealed to me that, even though Africans had indeed sold Africans into slavery, ultimately He was the victim.

He explained to me that He was victimized in Genesis in His dealings with Adam. He revealed it to me again in His dealings with David in 2 Samuel, and in the New Testament—through the Truth being manifested in one Person, Jesus.

There Is an Escape

Bound in fratricidal deception, man (since Cain) continues to kill his brother. All the wars and all the conflicts in history (in our personal lives as well) have their roots in Adam's and Cain's disobedience. Man's <u>disobedience</u> toward God is sin, but his attempts to <u>justify</u> his disobedience are iniquity. Man's way focuses on himself in his dealings with other <u>men</u> rather than upon the Sovereign <u>Creator</u> of all men. Cain refused to address his issues with his Creator; instead, he and all mankind since have implemented their own plan along their own path—in essence, doing what they want, when they want, the way they want.

How do we escape this fratricidal deception? Truth helped me answer this question as well. Both the Hutu Christians and the Tutsi Christians had their own reasons for annihilating each other—but the reasons were really excuses covering sin and iniquity. The deception that these two tribes bought into started with Adam and has continued down through history. Still, man repeatedly refuses to step back onto God's path, actually refusing to acknowledge His Sovereignty. The only escape for us is to accept God's offer to be restored to Him in friendship and in love through biblical reconciliation.

"Our Chooser Is Broke"

The entire population of the earth is divided into only two categories—the children of God and the children of the devil. You are either one or the other. *"By this you know the children of God and the children of the devil. The children of God love their brother, and they practice righteousness"*[3] (1 John 3:4-9).

Then the apostle John refers to Genesis and compares what we have in Christ with what we have in Cain: *"We know the children of God because they practice righteousness, and they love their brother, not as Cain who was of the wicked one and murdered his brother"*[4] (vv. 10-15). In other words, there are those who follow the path of God—the righteous— and those who follow the path of man—the iniquitous. The important thing is that each of us has been given the right and ability to choose which path we will take.

I recall an incident where I was sitting outside the door of a studio with two drug addicts, waiting to be interviewed by a radio talk show host. As we sat there, the two guys began talking with each other about their situations and what it was like to be addicted. It was a sad story. Eventually their conversation took a deeper turn. They discussed the emotional effect of the drugs and how they had to have more and more of the "stuff" to experience less and less satisfaction.

I knew enough about the problem to understand that they were referring to the chemical imbalance produced by drugs and how it inhibits one's ability to feel. The part of the brain relating to sensory perception is defective, numbed and deadened by the "drug of choice." But it was still their choice to pop those pills or shoot up—or not. Finally, one guy turned to the other and said, "You know, man, our chooser is broke."

Those words still echo in my head and in my heart. As I studied Genesis further, Cain's refusal to choose to reconcile with God frustrated me even more than those two addicts because Cain's choice has affected all of history since. I wanted to tell him, "Just talk to God; tell Him what you did, repent, and let man get back onto God's path." I wanted to make him see the faults in his attitude. I wanted to tell him, "You're leading multitudes to death and destruction. You can talk with God; you are so close to Him and can so easily step back onto His path." I could not understand how Cain could know the One True God and remain defiant. Then it became clear: We are all only one step away from choosing the wrong path or one step away from the opportunity to turn around and step back onto God's path.

Throughout history, bad, sinful, or otherwise unacceptable behavior has plagued humanity in every society—so much so, in fact, that wrongdoing has become an accepted, though unwelcome, part of every life. But mankind has an incredible ability to justify his worst actions, even while knowing they are wrong. Yet, he is unwilling and seemingly incapable of controlling himself.

The world could be an immeasurably better place in which to live if we would adopt that ultimate of life's purposes—to become our brother's keeper. Humanity's main focus, however, has forever been inward—upon itself—rather than upon its Creator. As a result, we find ourselves mired in an existence so deeply in competition and conflict with each other, that we must accept our situation—life on man's path results in ever-increasing depravity.

We Can't "Fix" It

I do not claim that man does not want to be good or to do good; I am convinced, however, that his attempts to "fix" himself have been woefully unrealistic and terribly ineffective. He continues to create laws, policies, and regulations in an attempt to control his destructive behavior, but senseless tragedies still occur.

On the tenth anniversary of the Columbine school shooting in Colorado, I read again a statement made to a special session of Congress by the father of one of the victims. In his powerful testimony, Darrell Scott said:

"Since the dawn of creation there has been both good and evil in the hearts of men and women. We all contain the seeds of kindness or the seeds of violence. The death of my wonderful daughter, Rachel Joy Scott, and the deaths of that heroic teacher and the other eleven children must not be in vain. Their blood cries out for answers.

"The first recorded act of violence was when Cain slew his brother Abel out in the field. The villain was not the club he used.... The true killer was Cain, and the reason for the murder could only be found in Cain's heart.

"In the days that followed the

Columbine tragedy, I was amazed at how quickly fingers were pointed...but much of the blame lies behind those pointed fingers.... We do not need more restrictive laws... No amount of gun laws can stop someone who spends months planning this kind of massacre. The real villain lies within our own hearts."

That statement struck me as truth from God. Our war is not with our brother. I see myself in Cain's defiance when I say no to God. I have not killed my brother, yet every time I refuse God's will and choose mine, I am on man's path. I also see myself in Eric and Dylan, the two boys who destroyed their classmates. I have not blasted away the lives of my colleagues, but when I speak a careless word or do not act in love, I am choosing man's path. But when I accept God's grace and mercy in forgiveness for my sin and iniquity, I am restored in friendship and love.

What if this is the truth that explains why we are the way we are? What if this is the solution? Whether we are willing to accept it or not, we are all in desperate need of deliverance—reconciliation with God. He Himself invites us: *"Come now, let us reason together...though your sins are as scarlet, they shall be as white as snow; though they are red like crimson, they shall be as wool"* (Isaiah 1:18).

> *" I find then a law,*
> *that evil is present with me,*
> *the one who wills to do good.*
> *For I delight in the law of God*
> *according to the inward man.*
> *But I see another law in my members,*
> *warring against the law of my mind,*
> *and bringing me into captivity*
> *to the law of sin which is in my members.*
> *O wretched man that I am!*
> *Who will deliver me from this body of death?"*
>
> *Romans 7:21-24*

5

DELIVERANCE: RECONCILED TO GOD!

SET FREE FROM BURDENS AND BLAME

*"For if when we were enemies of God
we were reconciled to God
through the death of His Son,
much more, having been reconciled,
we shall be saved by His life."*

ROMANS 5:10 NIV

How can warring tribes be reconciled? How is forgiveness possible when we have caused the death of our brother's future? Can we be delivered from this allegiance to evil? It is time to quit blaming each other and to begin reasoning with God.

When we could do nothing to help ourselves, God offered up His own Son who in obedience laid down His life so that we would know the truth. His message is first to *"love the Lord your God with all your heart, with all your soul, and with all your mind"* and then you will be able to *"love your neighbor as yourselves"* (Matt. 22:37, 39). God forgave you for killing His only Son. He died in your place so that together we could stop the cycle of killing each other.

With that arrangement in place,

who are we to refuse to accept His offer of reconciliation—being restored to His favor—and to extend that same forgiveness to others who have wronged us? Because of His sacrifice, Rwandans can forgive fellow Rwandans for doing what they did. Only by forgiving as we have been forgiven can we be truly free.

It is necessary for me to understand what God gave up in order to bring me back to His side and be reconciled to Him. God paid the ultimate price to deliver me from the slavery of sin.

People associate reconciliation with tribal and racial differences—all manner of personal conflicts—but these are mere distractions that cloud the real issue. Man is separated from his Creator and is, therefore, in need of reconciliation with Him.

Bondage is broken when the knowledge of truth allows freedom to take place in the mind and in the heart. It becomes immediately evident to the senses, the mind, and to subsequent perceptions. We are able to see that we were in darkness—literal ignorance. Ignorance of what? Ignorance of the deception that is the root cause of the issues of life.

We know truth comes from the Word of God. Jesus said, *"The Word became flesh and walked among us. And we beheld Him in all of His glory full of grace and truth"* (John 1:14). Jesus was full of grace (unmerited favor) and truth (the reality at the basis of the appearances of the issues of life). Finally we are able to see that Jesus is the Answer—the only Answer.

Jesus—the Way, the Truth, and the Life

A TV documentary, "Journey to the End of the Universe," reveals an immense creation in which we live all of life's experiences on a pinhead. That's mind-boggling! I can't relate to that. So God gives us a measure of faith because we can't imagine it, and He sends us Himself in human flesh—Jesus—to pluck us out of the mess we have made of things and to redeem our lives from the path of destruction we have chosen.

Salvation and restoration are demonstrated by this glorious God. Humanity was separated from our Creator, but He has made it possible for us to be "reconnected" with Him by reconciling through His Son. That gives us access to and relationship with Him. He has made Himself known through His unconditional love and justice, necessary because of our sinfulness. He chose to send His own Son to take away my sins, which is the ultimate demonstration of His grace and mercy. He made it possible for me to know who He is; we can have no doubts about His character. He even made it possible for me to have fellowship with Him so that all I can say at this point is, "GLORY!"

In John 14:6, Jesus further described His identity with the Father. *"I am the Way, the Truth, and the Life. No man comes to the Father but by Me."*

He says, *"I am the Way"*—if there is no way, there is no going.

He says, *"I am the Truth"*—if there is no truth, there is no knowing.

He says, *"I am the Life"*—if there is no life, there is no living.

This affirmation of Jesus is one of the greatest philosophical utterances of all time. He did not say He knew the way, the truth, and the life, nor did He merely teach these concepts. He did not make Himself the exponent of a new system; He simply declared Himself to be the final key to all mysteries. And His blood was spilled for us in the ultimate sacrifice of all time.

In Leviticus 17:11, God explains, *"For the life of a creature is in the blood, and I have given it to you to make atonement for yourselves on the altar; it is the blood that makes atonement for one's life."* God deals with us through the source of life (blood). You remember that it began with Adam and Eve when they tried to cover themselves with fig leaves to hide their nakedness. God gave them coats of skin; the atonement through the death of the animals (bloodshed) had been made. Where there is no shedding of blood, there is no remission of sin. This blood sacrifice is consistent from Genesis to Revelation.

After years of study, God helped me to understand. If we accept His plan and agree to do what He wants us to do, the way He wants us to do it, when He wants us to do it, the Holy Spirit and the Word begin to transform us into the image of Christ. In this way we become His disciples.

How Are We Discipled?

When we receive Jesus Christ as our Savior and are born again, we become children of God. From that point, we are taught from the Scriptures what happens next: *"Do not be conformed to this world, but be transformed by the renewing of your mind, that you may prove what is that good and acceptable and perfect will of God"* (Romans 12:1-2). We are *transformed* so that we can be *conformed* to the image of Christ through the knowledge of the Word of God, the guidance of the Holy Spirit, and the person who makes us a disciple.

As new believers, we continue the transformation into the image of Christ by reading the Word, developing a daily devotion and prayer time, and building a strong relationship and fellowship with God. In all of this, we rely on His Holy Spirit to mentor us and lead us into all truth.

When I was younger, I did not like church; I did not like preachers, either. I saw a lot of hypocrisy in the church—saw it as a social club. Today, I am a preacher who is in the process of helping plant a church. What happened? God changed me. I did not go to seminary; I just wanted to know the truth, so I allowed the Holy Spirit to be my Teacher and my Counselor. It is He who has brought me to where I am today.

Too often, we don't give the Holy Spirit enough credit. If we ask for wisdom and understanding, it is not refused us. However, we have to be willing to follow His leading. Once we come to Christ, the Holy Spirit is right there for us. He is the "Helper;" He is the one who comes alongside to help and guide us. We must allow Him to move in and take charge of our lives—to be the "Instructor" so that we can be the disciples who one day might teach others. And what is the curriculum? It's all about reconciliation. It's about receiving God's grace and then extending it to others, first to the Body of Christ.

Christ's Body—the Church

True believers become members of

the Body of Christ—the Church. It is the responsibility of the church to make disciples of its members and equip them for the work of the ministry. Church members must edify and encourage people to continue to grow and get involved with the work of winning the world back to God through Jesus Christ.

So many people look at the Church as the "end," but it is actually the means to the end. Not everyone is called to be a preacher, deacon, trustee, usher, choir member, or other infrastructure service provider for the church. According to Jesus' command, the Church is to equip believers for deployment into the world in order to reflect God's love within their sphere of influence. As they are sent into the seven social spheres of influence—education, government and politics, media and entertainment, social communities, religions and religious groups, sports, and business —they will impact the culture, ultimately leading people to salvation.

Unfortunately, the Church, in general, is operating in a paradigm where people are won to Christ and are brought to church every Sunday for the purpose of building strong memberships rather than creating disciples who will go out and win the earth back to the Lord. This gives Satan the opportunity to deceive people into thinking that only a handful of people are righteous enough to be ambassadors of God's love, sharing the blueprint for biblical reconciliation.

First the *Victim* Forgives

There is much more to reconciliation than simply having one person say, "I'm sorry," and another, "I forgive you." Just as God provided the way back to Himself while we were yet sinners, so the first step in remediating the bitterness that exists in the hearts of the Rwandans (and in every wounded heart in the world) is for the victim to initiate the cycle of forgiveness.

Today in Rwanda, the only release from hatred and bitterness occurs when each victim goes back to each perpetrator and initiates *reconciliation through forgiveness*. This properly allows the victim control of the process. There is no way to tell just how many individual cases there have been, but when members of the victims' families have found and forgiven the people who either ordered the killing or actually murdered their relatives, the results have been nothing short of amazing. By forgiving the perpetrators, the victims were able to release the hatred that otherwise caused stress, pressure, and tension. The process of forgiveness opens the door for the perpetrators of atrocities to repent and confess that what they have done is wrong.

Out of this process in Rwanda, a legal entity called the Gacaca Courts was born. Victims found the perpetrators, forgave them, and experienced release. The perpetrators of the atrocities repented, in turn asked for forgiveness, and as a result, healing and wholeness is well underway.

One of the most moving stories I have ever heard came from a mother who confronted the murderer of her son, who had been hacked to death with a machete. In the Gacaca Court one day, she forgave the killer.

Stunned by this believing woman's grace in spite of her loss, the man repented. "I'm really sorry I did that. Can you ever forgive me?"

She looked her son's killer right in the eye. "I'll forgive you...on one condition."

He frowned, not sure what to expect. "What is it?"

"I'll forgive you...if you'll be my son."

We have already seen this picture enacted on the Cross of Calvary. The great Creator God, victimized by our sin, willingly laid down His life in payment for our sins through Jesus Christ His Son. And that is not the end of the story. After we had finished killing His Son, the Father then invited all who would believe in Him to become His children. Amazing grace!

Make Peace, Not War

When I look at my true self—seen and unseen—I have to ask, "What is the reality at the basis of the appearance of the manifested veritable essence of me? What within me holds evil and such potential for violence? What do I share with all men that is ready in an instant to harm my brother instead of help him?"

The world is searching for peace, but

peace is not in the DNA of man. All we know is what we do exceptionally well—*make war*. Peace is in the DNA of those who have been born again—those who have been born of the *Prince of Peace*. Peace is elusive for those who do not know Truth. In Romans, Paul explains that we have been justified by faith. If we receive the message of truth from the Word of truth (through Jesus Christ) and receive Him as sovereign, we are restored to God in friendship and in love. Then we have peace through God (see Romans 5:1-2).

Since the Scriptures tell us that we have peace with God through Jesus Christ, we must have been at war with God. If we look at what is revealed from Genesis to Jesus, deception is exposed. Adam, in his disobedience, opened a path of iniquity that works contrary to God. This led to the depravity that resulted in the dilemma in which we find ourselves today. It reveals the need for deliverance that God made available through Jesus Christ before creation.

As a byproduct of the Rwandan experience, a small and interesting industry was birthed. Today, together, the victims and the perpetrators weave baskets, Tutsi and Hutu, working side by side in a peaceful paradigm. Not surprisingly, the baskets are called "peace baskets." Both sides are ultimately restored in friendship and in love, and the process has begun to grow and thrive throughout the land. Now each individual is careful to remember that it is his God-given responsibility to take care of his brother rather than to kill him.

Moving Out

I was drafted during the Viet Nam War. While in Fort Benning, Georgia, we received our orders to ship out. My duffel bag was packed and I, along with 1500 other American soldiers, was sitting in the street. We'd heard the buzz. GIs stepping on land mines in the jungle. Prisoners of war being tortured. Radio operators targeted first by snipers to shut down communications...I'd trained to be a radio operator....Suddenly I had to speak with my mom. As the major prayer warrior in the family, I needed to hear her voice one more time.

"Ma," I said, choking back tears. "We're leaving. We're on our way to Korea and then to Nam."

She didn't say anything for a moment. "Son," she spoke up finally, "I'm going to pray... right now!" After a brief pause, she hung up, and I knew she had hit her knees.

Thirty minutes later, the sergeant called off a list of nine names. Mine was among them. "Go back to the company area," he instructed. "You didn't get security clearance. You won't be going this time." Only nine out of fifteen hundred...what are the odds of that?

By the time I had transferred from the engineering unit to the bridge company, my time in the Army was up. I was discharged three months early...with an invitation to attend spring training with the Red Sox!

Daddy's training... Ma's prayers...

Even with a second chance at life, I was still on my own path in those years, trying to do what I wanted to do, when I wanted to do it, the way I wanted to do it. But I would soon come to understand that God was positioning me for His purposes, preparing me to play in the real Big Leagues. I was saved from death to serve Him for the rest of my life. The message was simple: First, be reconciled to God, then offer what I had been given—forgiveness and restoration.

"For by grace you have been saved
through faith, and that not of yourselves;
it is the gift of God, not of works,
lest anyone should boast.
For we are His workmanship,
created in Christ Jesus for good works,
which God prepared beforehand
that we should walk in them."

Ephesians 2:8-10

6

DEPLOYMENT:
SAVED TO SERVE

GOD'S STRATEGY—
THE ONLY SOLUTION FOR WORLD PEACE

*"Now all things are of God,
who has reconciled us
to Himself through Jesus Christ,
and has given us the ministry of reconciliation,
that is that God was in Christ
reconciling the world to Himself,
not imputing their trespasses to them,
and has committed to us
the word of reconciliation....
Now then, we are ambassadors for Christ."*

2 CORINTHIANS 5:18-20 NIV

In the early days of my youth spent with my family, I think we all knew our perfect, little world could not last forever. Each of us would eventually have to leave the nest and venture out into the real world to deal with its issues.

Some years later, integration began in earnest. Each of us had his unique set of circumstances. For me, it was the military and pro ball.

Some situations might have otherwise been traumatic, but thanks in large part to lessons we learned from Dad and Ma, we managed to do okay. So many of those earlier events have now become a clear prelude to what would happen much later in my life.

We Are God's Ambassadors

What would the world be like if we reconciled and maintained a strong "vertical" relationship with God? What would the world be like if we took it upon ourselves to care for each other and not kill each other?

In Paul's second letter to the Corinthians, believers are called "ambassadors for Christ" (5:21). God was in Christ reconciling and restoring the world to Himself in friendship and love. In this role, believers are to tell the world that the first Adam's sin separated us *from* God, while Jesus Christ, the last Adam, died to reconcile us *to* God.

> *Now all things are of God, who has reconciled us to Himself through Jesus Christ, and has given us the ministry of reconciliation, that is, that God was in Christ reconciling the world to Himself, not imputing their trespasses to them, and has committed to us the word of reconciliation. Now then, we are ambassadors for Christ, as though God were pleading through us: we implore*

you on Christ's behalf, be reconciled to God. For He made Him who knew no sin to be sin for us, that we might become the righteousness of God in Him. (II Corinthians 5:18-21)

Now it is up to us to mirror the same love, justice, grace, and mercy that He uses in our deliverance. Jesus explained the reason for our purpose this way, *"So that they all may be one, as You, Father, are in Me, and I in You; that they also may be one in Us, that the world may believe that You sent Me"* (John 17:21).

It is through our reconciliation with God and our acceptance of our role as ambassadors that God is revealed to the world. His presence is manifested in our daily submission and obedience to Him and our love for our brothers.

As believers, we are to be peacemakers. We are to practice the righteousness of God through Jesus Christ. We are deployed to teach this and to model reconciliation as a walk of peace in our daily lives. This path of reconciliation, peace, and restoration will contrast sharply with the world's path of confrontation, conflict, and war. As believers who act as one in the Body of Christ, we will demonstrate the same kind of love and mercy we have received—at home and around the world.

Into All the World

One question I had asked God as a ten-year-old boy, however, remained to be answered: "Why did we have to come here as slaves?"

At a conference in Richmond, Virginia, in 1994, while the Rwandan crisis was in full sway, I met a man who would play a part in answering my childhood question. Romain Zannou, pastor to the president of Benin, told me that he had had the privilege of leading the president of that African nation to the Lord.

Discovering that we shared the same heart for the lost peoples of the world, especially in the area of reconciliation with God, we remained in communication for the next two years.

In October of 1996, Pastor Zannou called me from Benin. "Jack," he said, "today God has placed a heavy burden upon my church for what my ancestors did to your ancestors by selling them into slavery." As we talked, we felt as if we were speaking on behalf of generations of people. He was speaking for all of the people who had sold us into slavery, and I, on behalf of all those (on this side of the world) who were sold. We agreed that he should come to America to offer an apology for what his ancestors had done to ours. I would arrange speaking engagements in some of the African-American churches here.

Prior to that, two friends of mine, Brian Johnson and George Thomas, and I would attend a large World Evangelization Conference in South Africa. Pastor Zannou would meet us there for further discussion of his plans to come to our country.

Through a series of God-ordained events in South Africa, Brian Johnson and I were summoned to Johannesburg to meet with the president of Benin. Our problem was that we didn't have transportation from Pretoria, where I was staying, to the capital city. Before we knew it, we had received an offer from the pastor of the Central Baptist Church of

Pretoria, a very distinguished gentleman, to drive us there.

It was the strangest feeling. Here we were—two African-Americans—sitting in the back seat of a brand-new Mercedes-Benz, being chauffeured by a white, South African pastor and his assistant! Not only that, but they were escorting us to meet with a black pastor and the president of Benin. I looked over at Brian and whispered, "This has got to be God!"

When we arrived, security personnel met us and ushered us upstairs to meet President Matthieu Kerekou. Our chat lasted about an hour and a half. During that time, President Kerekou shared his experiences growing up in colonized Benin, and we told him how it was growing up as African-Americans. It was the president's idea to develop a Reconciliation Conference in his home country, where he would make a public apology for what his ancestors had done to ours. We also invited him to come to America to attend the National Prayer Breakfast. While here, he could speak to various churches in the area and offer his formal apology.

Little did we know what would happen as an outcome of that historic meeting. That an entire movement would be set in motion that would circle the globe.

"We Forgive It All!"

In February of 1999, President Matthieu Kerekou was finally able to come to Washington. We had arranged for him to speak to the congregations of two churches in order to make his petition of forgiveness. It was at the second church that a powerful scenario took place.

The president got down on one knee before the pastor and more than 1500 other people in that church. He stated that he deeply regretted what had happened all those years ago and that he was sorry for the sins of his ancestors. In reply, the pastor, Bishop David Parrin, made an equally profound statement of forgiveness. "You ask me to forgive you and your ancestors for having put us in a position where we had to experience only the 'second best' in everything?" he began. "You ask us to forgive you for everything that has been done to us for all these years because of the color of our skin? Because of the finished work of Jesus Christ and because of our faith in His finished work, we forgive it all!"

Such a spirit of brokenness moved through the entire church at that moment that even the Secret Servicemen, who were strategically placed about the auditorium in order to protect the president, were in tears behind their dark glasses. The Conference of Reconciliation had taken place; the Reconciliation Ceremony was finished. Or was it?

After that amazing time, the president issued a challenge to continue the process. We were invited to come to Benin to work with a committee to plan another conference in his country before the year 2000. In April, a delegation from America met with his committee for nine days, twelve hours each day, to strategize as to how to maximize the effectiveness of the conference.

It finally took place in December, 1999, just days before the turn of the century. President Kerekou had invited 125 representatives from a delegation of African-

Americans (for which I was responsible), along with 25 delegates from Europe and South America, regional chiefs and kings, the president of Ghana, Jerold Rawlins, as well as Georgina Dufoix, the French Minister of Family Affairs. All of us came together in a spirit of reconciliation. All of us offered apologies, and those of us of the African-American Diaspora made a statement of forgiveness. This entire process created the platform by which we could apply the biblical principles of reconciliation.

Following the conference, what else could be done after the crying, and the hugging, and the apologies were over? Biblical principles of reconciliation were put into place, which opened the door to forgiveness and repentance which, in turn, gave rise to reconciliation. Relationships were built, and as a result, partnerships were established. Socio-economic development then took place, and communities were built, where each individual became his brother's keeper and not his brother's killer.

"Why Are You Doing This?"

At the time, President Kerekou had been personally supporting five missionaries in a remote village called Akpali. These missionaries were taught that when they went into a village, they were initially to say nothing at all about Jesus. They were simply to work and build relationships with the people.

If a farmer got sick, they would work the farm for him until he was well. If the farmer's wife had a child, the missionaries' wives would take care of the new mother until she was back on her feet. As a result of these actions, the question would eventually be asked, "Why are you doing this?"

It was then that they were taught to say, "We do this because we have a debt of love that we owe." The next question "What is this debt of love?" would be the missionaries' invitation to share the gospel of Jesus Christ. As a result of that strategy, of four hundred people in that village, four hundred were saved! These people not only heard the gospel, they saw it demonstrated in their lives. That was the beginning of the process that resulted from the Reconciliation Conference. Other projects quickly followed.

Adopt-a-Village

After the conference, much thought was given to what else might be done to further enhance the process of reconciliation. As African-American pastors returned to Benin and were introduced to chiefs in several villages—the same chiefs who may very well have been direct descendents of people who sold their ancestors into slavery—a novel idea emerged. It was decided that some of the pastors would "adopt" entire villages and their congregations back home would support them in various ways.

After one pastor adopted a village, his church has, among other things, provided $10,000 for the installation of a well for clean water, $5,000 start-up funds for a micro bank, $30,000 for a new school, and $18,000 for a new clinic—all this by one group of people whose ancestors could possibly have been sold into slavery by the very ones they were so dedicated to helping. The reconciliation process has brought peace as well as a "reconnection" in the lives of the people from that church.

Another village, Yawa, was home to two separate factions—one group hated the other because their ancestors had stolen people from the other group and sold them into slavery to the Europeans. An unexpected and very special blessing from the reconciliation conference came when a delegation of African-Americans from the Baltimore region agreed to visit Yawa. Both factions from this village wanted to hear from the descendents of those who had been stolen and sold. The visitors were able to speak peace directly into a situation that had been tense for the previous 400 years. The value of reconciliation could easily be seen as it brought peace to an otherwise volatile region.

Pastors continue to visit Benin and are still being introduced in villages that many of them ultimately adopt. They are finding that when the biblical principles of reconciliation are implemented, an emotional barrier comes down and people are able to get to know and begin to feel comfortable with each other. Then that sequence of partnership, socio-economic development, and community building can begin.

For example, those throughout the world who once were victimized by their African brothers have now become friends and partners. Assistance of all types may now be offered to aid in many of their issues, and they can begin to assist us in some of ours as well. A whole new level of communication is reached, and once unknown truths about each other may finally be uncovered.

Equipped with this understanding, I am able to see what happened in Rwanda. Now I have answers as to why the Hutu and the Tutsi killed each other as they did. When that modern-day holocaust in Rwanda finally ended, I realized the reasons they had for doing what they did were only camouflage, intended to disguise and hide the fact that they, like so many others down through history, had been tragically deceived. Their war was never with their brother. Their conflicts (like all of man's conflicts) were with God. Once aware of this fact, they, alone, could not deal with the emotions that genocide had caused. The only correct way they could deal with them was by practicing the biblical principles of reconciliation.

The ultimate lesson lies in the realization that it is better—safer, more practical, and mutually profitable—to be one's keeper than one's killer.

What Would *You* Do?

In 286 A.D., a legion of soldiers from Thebes, on a mission to conquer the people of Gaul (France), illustrated this principle when they took a stand and refused to kill fellow Christians.

After their victory, Emperor Maximilian of Rome issued an order that the whole army should join in offering sacrifices to the Roman gods for the success of their mission. Participation in the sacrifices, which involved killing Christians, would also recognize the emperor's claim to divinity. The Theban Legion withdrew itself, encamped near Aguanum, and refused to take part in these rites.

When this news reached Maximilian,

he repeatedly commanded them to obey his orders. At their refusal, he ordered that every tenth man be put to death. A second "decimation" was ordered unless the men obeyed the order given, but throughout the legion camp, they all declared that they would never allow themselves to carry out such a sacrilegious order.

When the emperor heard this news, he ordered the second decimation to be carried out. Yet they still maintained their resolve. After the second decimation, Maximilian warned the remainder of the Theban legion that if they persisted in their disobedience, not a man among them would be able to escape death.

Led by Maurice, the Theban Legion sent this letter as a reply to Maximilian's order:

> Emperor, we are your soldiers but also the soldiers of the true God. We owe you military service and obedience, but we cannot renounce Him who is our Creator and Master, and also yours, even though you reject Him. In all things which are not against His law, we most willingly

obey you, as we have done hitherto. We readily oppose your enemies whoever they are, but we cannot stain our hands with the blood of innocent people (Christians). We had taken an oath to God before we took one to you; you cannot place any confidence in our second oath if we violate the first. You commanded us to execute Christians; behold we are such. We confess God the Father, the Creator of all things, and His Son, Jesus Christ, God. We have seen our comrades slain with the sword; we do not weep for them, but rather rejoice at their honor. Neither this, nor any other provocation has tempted us to revolt. Behold, we have arms in our hands, but we do not resist, because we would rather die innocent than live by any sin.[1]

When Maximilian heard this, he realized that these men were determined to remain in their Christian faith, and he despaired of being able to turn them from their steadfast position. He, therefore, decreed, in a final sentence, that they should be rounded up and slaughtered. The troops sent to execute this order came to the blessed legion and drew their swords upon those holy men who, for the love of life, did not refuse to die. They were all slain with the sword. They never resisted in any way. Putting aside their weapons, they offered their necks to the executioners. Neither their numbers nor the strength of arms tempted them to uphold the justice of their cause by force. As a result, many of those troops who were sent to execute the Emperor's order were won to Christianity by the actions of these brave men.

I would have never understood the devotion displayed before the world by the Theban Legion or the forgiveness shown by massacred survivors if God had not revealed His perspective to me. What began for me so many years ago as a ten-year-old boy seeking answers from God has become a lifelong journey. He has shown Himself to me, one step at a time. He has slowly prepared me to fully understand the potential of life as a member of the Body of Christ. I had to understand all of the details, from the full impact of iniquity and Adam's disobedience to the amazing freedom found in reconciliation.

In the wonder of his awesome love, mercy and grace, I am now able to see that I have no choice but to glorify Him. Because of His mercy toward me, I have no choice but to forgive others!

One Last Word

As a believer, my job is to be about reconciliation—letting the world know that the God of glory has restored me to Him in friendship and love. My bent toward sin and rebellion—its origin going all the way back to the Garden—is what makes my war with God an ongoing one. Conflict with Him makes restoration essential. God made it known that He was my primary enemy, but He has also revealed that He has done everything necessary to restore my relationship with Him in friendship and love. He is now, in fact, my primary source of peace. When that plan is received and understood, His desire is that I communicate that message—the Good News, the Gospel—to as many people throughout the world as possible.

The way I carry myself speaks volumes when it comes to the world's understanding of what God has done. It is important that others see this so that they might make the only right decision. In the book of John, Jesus said, *"God, I pray that they will be one as You and I are one"*...why?... *"so the world will know that You sent me."*

It is the love we have for one another that will be the most power-filled message as to why God sent Jesus. What God has done, therefore, on my behalf, enables me to practice the humility that is required to live in peace. The same message is extended to you. Receive it, appreciate it, and know God's power as well as His will for all mankind.

God continues His conversations with me, patiently teaching me and constantly reconciling Himself to me. I continue to let His love, mercy, and grace flow through me for others to see.

It has taken me a lifetime to uncover the answer to my childhood question about why my people were sold as slaves. Our brothers sold us because they did not know the truth. They were deceived into thinking that we were the enemy, but they were really at war with God. They trusted in their passions rather than in their Creator. Yet even in their wrong conclusions, God still had mercy on them and on me.

When I sought Him out, He reconciled me to Himself. I also learned that if I am reconciled to God, and my brother—black, white, Hispanic, Asian, or otherwise—is reconciled to God, then I have no choice but to be reconciled to my brother. And so I have determined my life's path—to be my brother's keeper,

In my youth I was a Big League pitcher, but that position did not come without consistent hard work and determination. I am humbled by what God has allowed me to accomplish in my lifetime—but more excited about what the future holds as He directs me to speak the message of reconciliation throughout the world.

Those who wanted me dead did not know that God had a better plan. I am back now to tell them and all the warring tribes the answer. I am here to reveal the wonderment, the joy, the anticipation of the hope and the future that God has in store for them.

I am here to forgive. And that is the most powerful, life-changing message on the planet. Jesus' last words before His crucifixion are my mandate: *"Father, forgive them, for they know not what they do."* If we follow His lead, the world will never be the same.

"Now all things are of God,
who has reconciled us to
Himself through Jesus Christ,
and has given us the ministry of reconciliation,
that is, that God was in Christ
reconciling the world to Himself,
not imputing their trespasses to them,
and has committed to us
the word of reconciliation.
Now then, we are ambassadors for Christ,
as though God were pleading through us:
we implore you on Christ's behalf,
be reconciled to God. "

2 Corinthians 5:18-20

Appendix A

BIBLICAL RECONCILIATION MODEL

I. If true reconciliation is going to take place, it must be initiated by the victim. The victim initiates forgiveness which is intended to cause remorse and sorrow for the perpetrator. The perpetrator must then acknowledge sorrow for his actions.

II. From that point, they can be reconciled--restored in friendship and love. Only then will they be able to discuss the actions perpetrated and their negative impact. Thereafter, discussion can take place about those steps that might be taken in order to keep those negative actions from recurring. That, in turn, will allow both parties to establish genuine relationships that are based on trust.

III. The positive outcome is that they can then establish genuine partnerships where projects can be initiated to stimulate socio-economic development. Tangible benefits can then be reaped from those partnerships.

IV. The ultimate result is realized when communities are built where inhabitants can become their brother's keeper rather than their brother's killer. These results can be witnessed wherever Biblical Reconciliation is practiced.

Appendix B

TESTIMONIALS

The Adopt-a-Village Initiative and COMINAD are direct results of reconciliation and the rebuilding of relationships from the Benin Conference.

Adopt-A-Village Program
Yawa Village Project, Inc.
Annual Pan African Festival
Pan African Collective

My involvement with Africa actually dates to the summer of 1971 when I served as a volunteer with Operation Crossroads Africa, a cultural exchange program headquartered in New York, which for over a half century has sent ten thousand persons to Africa, largely to participate in rural development projects. The founder of Crossroads was the late Dr. James H. Robinson, a visionary pastor of a church in Harlem who while perhaps never using the word *reconciliation* to describe the mission and work of the organization, nonetheless recognized the need to build bridges of understanding between people of diverse races and cultures. That summer, working alongside white and other black students from across America, and Nigerian counterparts, afforded me a unique, unforgettable opportunity that certainly sparked an interest in me to contribute in some way to further the ideals of Dr. Robinson.

After graduating from the Harvard Business School in 1975, I led a group for Crossroads to Nigeria during the summer, and in 1977, became their Director of Development for three years, spending considerable time in remote villages throughout Africa. I subsequently worked for two other organizations that kept me intimately involved in reconciliation (while at the time never using that word to describe what I was engaged in) and human development, the African-American Institute and the Service and Development Agency (SADA), the latter being the global development arm of the African Methodist Episcopal Church.

I assumed the pastorate of Greater Mt. Nebo A.M.E. Church, located in Bowie, MD in 1988, and building upon my previous experiences in Africa, led two mission trips to West Africa in the early 1990s. However, upon meeting Jack Gaines, along with Brian Johnson, a long-term missionary to Africa, in 1998, my engagement with the concept of reconciliation became more focused. I attended an historic conference on reconciliation and community development sponsored by the Government of Benin in 1999, which led me to explore other ways for me and our church to pursue this vision of bringing people together for the sake of global health and development.

Jack and Brian introduced the Adopt-A-Village program to our church and the congregation embraced it enthusiastically. Since 2002, we have developed a vibrant relationship with the people of Yawa, a village in Benin, approximately three hours (by road) from the capital of Cotonou. Over forty members of our church have visited Yawa through four separate trips, including a group comprised of health professionals who held workshops with the villagers to empower them to promote better health care among themselves. We also provided financial support for the construction of the first school in the village, and we continue to help underwrite teacher salaries and the tuition cost for many of the students whose parents cannot afford the expense.

For us, this relationship is hardly one-sided. We are blessed by knowing that the people of Yawa are praying for us, individually as well as for the church collectively. Moreover, for those who have visited Yawa, they now have a global sensitivity beyond anything they could have imagined prior to this exposure.

Two years ago our church created the Yawa Village Project, Inc., a 501(c)(3) organization, whose purpose is to promote the ideals of reconciliation and development, using our partnership with Yawa as the impetus and stimulus for this effort. Additionally, since 2001, Greater Mt. Nebo has sponsored an annual Pan African Festival on the grounds of the church, drawing thousands each year from the Washington metropolitan area, to promote better understanding amongst people, especially with those representing the African Diaspora. Finally, in 2008, we established the Pan African Collective, an organization comprised of churches in the Washington area, and members of the African and Caribbean Diplomatic Corps, to foster relationships between these groups, again around the themes of reconciliation and development.

Much of what we are doing as a church as it relates to this reconciliation movement is directly attributable to the people who have influenced me in this regard, most notably Dr. James Robinson, Jack Gaines, and Brian Johnson, all of whom I mentioned earlier, the former President of Benin, Matthieu Kerekou, and the current Ambassador of Benin to the United States, Cyrille Oguin. It certainly is our hope that many more churches across this nation will become involved in this life-changing endeavor.

~Rev. Jonathan Weaver
Pastor, Greater Mount Nebo
African Methodist
Episcopal Church

COMINAD

From the start of the COMINAD network, our goal has been to create a vehicle that will reconcile Christians with one another, and to help people around the world reconcile with God and each other. We believe that the absence of reconciliation between man and God is the one cause for man not being reconciled to one another.

We have traveled to countries with the purpose of embracing people groups who were experiencing problems relating with people of other groups. Our focus was to facilitate reconciliation among these groups. An example of this type of reconciliation intervention occurred when we went to the small West African country of Benin.

We heard that there was a major problem between tribes that had the capability of flaring up into great violence if not attended to. The problem derived from animosity between the descendants of the people whose forefathers had captured men, women and children from other tribes. Their forefathers sold these people to white slave traders, who in turn transported them to the Americas. It was our privilege to sit with the people from tribal groups whose ancestors had sold people into slavery and those whose ancestors were sold. We experienced, first hand, the anger that began hundreds of years ago, yet remained fresh in the hearts of the people. We heard people cry out with great intensity, the extent in which they hated each other. The amazing thing for us was seeing the close proximity in which these antagonists lived. In some cases they lived in the same villages, as was the case with our first mediation encounter.

We found out rather quickly that we as

African-Americans had a role to play in reconciling some of the people of Africa who had been having major problems amongst themselves concerning the slave trade. We pleaded with both groups in the name of Christ Jesus to forgive one another's ancestors and to overcome the hatred that was in their hearts stemming from the slave trade. We were amazed that the people did forgive one another. Through our intervention, communities are now working together in a new reconciled paradigm, creating prosperity and happiness among the people in parts of that small country. We are also working in other countries and in the United States connecting people to God and each other for the purpose of salvation and prosperity.

~Mr. Brian Johnson
National Coordinator
COMINAD

ADOPT-A-VILLAGE

The Adopt-a-Village Initiative is a direct result of reconciliation and the rebuilding of relationships from the Benin Conference.

Since an initial visit to Benin, Africa, in July 2001, and seeing first hand that many villages lacked many basic needs, God moved me to adopt two villages for First Baptist Church Denbigh. Adoption of these villages meant that we would be committed to helping the villagers to have a better quality of life. During conversations with leaders of the villages, I learned that their most pressing needs were schools to educate their people and clean drinking water. Returning to my church congregation with the results of my visit and what I had committed to do, they readily agreed to helping the people of the villages.

To date, we have provided the villagers with books written in French, English, and Fong (in partnership with Hampton University), established a micro banking system; constructed and dedicated a well, a school, and a medical facility; provided motorcycles for the missionaries; and will be dedicating a 300-seat worship facility in May. While most of the funds for these projects have been provided by the First Baptist Church Denbigh family, we have had some assistance from Pastor David Spratley (Rising Sun Baptist Church, Lackey, Virginia), Pastor Sammie Simmons (St. Marks Four Bridges and Bethesda Baptist Churches, Sumpter, South Carolina), Pastor Ray Brown (Resurrection Baptist Church, San Antonio, Texas), and other individuals.

It is my prayer and hope that God will move upon the hearts of local pastors to catch the vision to adopt other villages, thereby helping to alleviate poverty, illiteracy, and disease for the villagers. With their adoption of other villages, local pastors will also be afforded the opportunity to spread the gospel of Jesus Christ.

Reverend Jack Gaines is a personal friend of mine, who has accompanied me on several tours of Africa and has seen first hand, what has been accomplished in our adopted villages and what still is lacking in many other villages.

We are looking forward to continuing our relationship and partnership with the country of Benin, Africa.

To God Be the Glory!

> ~Pastor Ivan T. Harris
> First Baptist Church, Denbigh
> http://www.fbcdenbigh.org/

ADOPT-A-VILLAGE

In 2002 I was exposed to the Reconciliation Ministry that was happening in the Republic of Benin. At the same time I heard about the Adopt-a-Village Program that was being initiated in that country also.

In 2003 I recruited three small teams to go to Benin. One team went in June, another in August, and another in October. The June team was a general exposure group that specialized in prayer and intercession. The latter two teams were exposed to the Adopt-a-Village Program.

The team members were exposed to certain villages that were selected by the local missionaries. The team was able to interact with the villagers by giving their testimonies. The villagers also sang, danced, and gave their testimonies to the team. This interaction brought the teams and the villagers together in sort of a kindred, bonding spirit. There was a sense that the team members from the States were distant family members of those in the villages. Consequently the team's interaction with the villagers was like a family reunion with relatives that had never seen each other before.

The villagers prayed for the team members, their families, and their churches. The team members sought to discover what were the greatest challenges that the villagers were facing. Most of the challenges that the villagers expressed were in this order: clean water, health care, education, and funding for small business initiatives.

The team members from the West became burdened by one or more challenges that the villagers had and voluntarily connected themselves with a particular village. The team members took many pictures of the villagers to show to their congregations and friends in the United States.

When the team members returned home, they showed the pictures of the villagers to their respective churches and small ministry groups. This resulted in individuals in the churches developing an affinity with the individuals in the villages.

From this cross-cultural communication, churches of team members began to officially adopt the village the team member displayed. Church members would begin to pray for their village regularly and to support the various projects they chose.

As a result of the Adopt-a-Village Program, I have taken teams to Benin every year since 2003. The churches of the team members have purchased wells, school materials, given funds for small business loans, and have supplied many other needs.

Some individuals in the States, who heard the report of the Adopt-a-Village Program committed themselves to adopt a village even before they visited the country.

We are also finding that most of the individuals, who come to the villages in Benin from the States, return one or more times to the village they have adopted. Thus these individuals maintain an on-going relationship with their village, and keep their church members involved.

~Virgil Lee Amos
General Director
Ambassadors Fellowship,
(a mission agency that ministers
in Latin America, Europe, South,
and East Asia, and Africa.)

Endnotes

Chapter 1

1. PBS Frontline documentary, April 2, 2004.
   http://news.bbc.co.uk/2/hi/programmes/panorama/3582011.
   stm

2. Paul Williams, M.D., "Eyewitness Account
   of Hutu Refugee Camps in Goma, Zaire (Congo),"
   1994.

3. *NAS New Testament Greek Lexicon*,
   Strong's #225.

4. *World Book Encyclopedia*, s.v. "veritable."

5. http://en.wikipedia.org/wiki/Qur'an

6. http.//en.wikipedia.org/wiki/Old_Testament

7. http://en.wikipedia.org/wiki/New_ Testament

8. Georgina Dufoix, Former French
   Minister of Family Affairs, in a speech to
   the National Prayer Breakfast,
   Washington, D.C., February 2, 2009.

Chapter 2

1. Hebrews 9:17-22

*"For a testament is in force after men are dead, since it
has no power at all while the testator lives. Therefore not
even the first covenant was dedicated without blood. For
when Moses had spoken every precept to all the people*

according to the law, he took the blood of calves and goats, with water, scarlet wool, and hyssop, and sprinkled both the book itself and all the people, saying, 'This is the blood of the covenant which God has commanded you.'

"Then likewise he sprinkled with blood both the tabernacle and all the vessels of the ministry. And according to the law almost all things are purified with blood, and without shedding of blood there is no remission."

2. Genesis 4:1-15

Cain Murders Abel

"Now Adam knew Eve his wife, and she conceived and bore Cain, and said, 'I have acquired a man from the LORD.' Then she bore again, this time his brother Abel. Now Abel was a keeper of sheep, but Cain was a tiller of the ground. And in the process of time it came to pass that Cain brought an offering of the fruit of the ground to the LORD. Abel also brought of the firstborn of his flock and of their fat. And the LORD respected Abel and his offering, but He did not respect Cain and his offering. And Cain was very angry, and his countenance fell.

"So the LORD said to Cain, 'Why are you angry? And why has your countenance fallen? If you do well, will you not be accepted? And if you do not do well, sin lies at the door. And its desire is for you, but you should rule over it.' Now Cain talked with Abel his brother; and it came to pass, when they were in the field, that Cain rose up against Abel his brother and killed him. Then the LORD said to Cain, 'Where is Abel your brother?' He said, 'I do not know. Am I my brother's keeper?'

"And He said, 'What have you done? The voice of your brother's blood cries out to Me from the ground. So now you are cursed from the earth, which has opened its mouth to receive your brother's blood from your hand. When you till the ground, it shall no longer yield its strength to you. A fugitive and a vagabond you shall be on the earth.' And Cain said to the LORD, 'My punishment is greater than I can bear! Surely You have driven me out this day from the face of the ground; I shall be hidden from Your face; I shall be a fugitive and a vagabond on the earth, and it will happen that anyone who finds me will kill me.'

"And the LORD said to him, 'Therefore, whoever kills Cain, vengeance shall be taken on him sevenfold.' And the LORD set a mark on Cain, lest anyone finding him should kill him."

3. For further reading: "Rwandan Conflict: Hutu and Tutsi History" http://www.historyplace.com/ worldhistorygenocide/rwanda.htm http://orvillejenkins.com/peoples/ tutsiandhutu.html

4. Phil Clark, "When the Killers Go Home," *Dissent*. www.dissentmagazine.org

Chapter 3

1. From http://en.wikipedia.org/depravity

2. Greg Brecht, "The World's Worst Massacres." http://www.globalwebpost.com/ genocide1971/articles/general/ worstmassacres.htm; http://en.wikipedia.org/w/ index.php?title=listofwarsand disastersbydeathtoll&printable=yes

3. TV interview with General Romeo Dallaire.
   www.pbs.org/wgbh/pages/frontline/
   shows/ghosts/interviews/dallaire.htm

4. John 4:1-4; Galatians 1:21; Nahum 1:2-8

5. 2 Samuel 11: 1-17
   David, Bathsheba, and Uriah

"It happened in the spring of the year, at the time when kings go out to battle, that David sent Joab and his servants with him, and all Israel; and they destroyed the people of Ammon and besieged Rabbah. But David remained at Jerusalem.

"Then it happened one evening that David arose from his bed and walked on the roof of the king's house. And from the roof he saw a woman bathing, and the woman was very beautiful to behold. So David sent and inquired about the woman. And someone said, 'Is this not Bathsheba, the daughter of Eliam, the wife of Uriah the Hittite?' Then David sent messengers, and took her; and she came to him, and he lay with her, for she was cleansed from her impurity; and she returned to her house. And the woman conceived; so she sent and told David, and said, 'I am with child.'

"Then David sent to Joab, saying, 'Send me Uriah the Hittite.' And Joab sent Uriah to David. When Uriah had come to him, David asked how Joab was doing, and how the people were doing, and how the war prospered. And David said to Uriah, 'Go down to your house and wash your feet.'" So Uriah departed from the king's house, and a gift of food from the king followed him. But Uriah slept at the door of the king's house with all the servants of his lord, and did not go down to his

house. So when they told David, saying, 'Uriah did not go down to his house,' David said to Uriah, "'Did you not come from a journey? Why did you not go down to your house?'

"And Uriah said to David, 'The ark and Israel and Judah are dwelling in tents, and my lord Joab and the servants of my lord are encamped in the open fields. Shall I then go to my house to eat and drink, and to lie with my wife? As you live, and as your soul lives, I will not do this thing.'

"Then David said to Uriah, 'Wait here today also, and tomorrow I will let you depart.' So Uriah remained in Jerusalem that day and the next. Now when David called him, he ate and drank before him; and he made him drunk. And at evening he went out to lie on his bed with the servants of his lord, but he did not go down to his house.

"In the morning it happened that David wrote a letter to Joab and sent it by the hand of Uriah. And he wrote in the letter, saying, 'Set Uriah in the forefront of the hottest battle, and retreat from him, that he may be struck down and die.' So it was, while Joab besieged the city, that he assigned Uriah to a place where he knew there were valiant men. Then the men of the city came out and fought with Joab. And some of the people of the servants of David fell; and Uriah the Hittite died also."

6. Psalm 51: 1-14

"Have mercy upon me, O God, according to Your lovingkindness; according to the multitude of Your tender mercies, Blot out my transgressions. Wash me thoroughly from my iniquity, and cleanse me from

my sin. For I acknowledge my transgressions, And my sin is always before me.

"Against You, You only, have I sinned, And done this evil in Your sight— That You may be found just when You speak, and blameless when You judge. Behold, I was brought forth in iniquity, and in sin my mother conceived me. Behold, You desire truth in the inward parts, And in the hidden part You will make me to know wisdom. Purge me with hyssop, and I shall be clean; wash me, and I shall be whiter than snow. Make me hear joy and gladness, that the bones You have broken may rejoice. Hide Your face from my sins, and blot out all my iniquities. Create in me a clean heart, O God, and renew a steadfast spirit within me. Do not cast me away from Your presence, and do not take Your Holy Spirit from me. Restore to me the joy of your salvation, and uphold me by your generous Spirit. Then I will teach transgressors your ways, and sinners shall be converted to You. Deliver me from the guilt of bloodshed, O God, The God of my salvation, and my tongue shall sing aloud of Your righteousness."

7. Acts 13: 22-24

"And when He [God] had removed him [Saul], He raised up for them David as king, to whom also He gave testimony and said, 'I have found David the son of Jesse, a man after My own heart, who will do all My will. From this man's seed, according to the promise, God raised up for Israel a Savior—Jesus— after John had first preached, before His coming, the baptism of repentance to all the people of Israel."

Chapter 4

1. The Reconciliation and Development Corporation was formed as a result of this conference and continues the work of restoring relationships. http://www.radcorp.org/

2. Darrell Scott's testimony before the House Judiciary Committee's subcomittee, May,1999.http://urbanlegends.about.com/ library/blldarrellscott.htm

3. Romans 7:15-24 (NIV

"I do not understand what I do. For what I want to do I do not do, but what I hate I do. And if I do what I do not want to do, I agree that the law is good. As it is, it is no longer I myself who do it, but it is sin living in me. I know that nothing good lives in me, that is, in my sinful nature. For I have the desire to do what is good, but I cannot carry it out. For what I do is not the good I want to do; no, the evil I do not want to do—this I keep on doing. Now if I do what I do not want to do, it is no longer I who do it, but it is sin living in me that does it. "So I find this law at work: When I want to do good, evil is right there with me. For in my inner being I delight in God's law; but I see another law at work in the members of my body, waging war against the law of my mind and making me a prisoner of the law of sin at work within my members. What a wretched man I am! Who will rescue me from this body of death? Thanks be to God—through Jesus Christ our Lord! "So then, I myself in my mind am a slave to God's law, but in the sinful nature a slave to the law of sin."

4. 1 John 3 4-15

"Whoever commits sin also commits lawlessness, and sin is lawlessness. And you know that He was manifested to take away our sins, and in Him there is no sin. Whoever abides in Him does not sin. Whoever sins has neither seen Him nor known Him.

"Little children, let no one deceive you. He who practices righteousness is righteous, just as He is righteous. He who sins is of the devil, for the devil has sinned from the beginning. For this purpose the Son of God was manifested, that He might destroy the works of the devil. Whoever has been born of God does not sin, for His seed remains in him; and he cannot sin, because he has been born of God.

"So then, I myself in my mind am a slave to God's law, but in the sinful nature a slave to the law of sin.

"In this the children of God and the children of the devil are manifest: Whoever does not practice righteousness is not of God, nor is he who does not love his brother. For this is the message that you heard from the beginning, that we should love one another, [12]not as Cain who was of the wicked one and murdered his brother. And why did he murder him? Because his works were evil and his brother's righteous.

"Do not marvel, my brethren, if the world hates you. We know that we have passed from death to life, because we love the brethren. He who does not love his brother abides in death. Whoever hates his brother is a murderer, and you know that no murderer has eternal life abiding in him."

Chapter 6

1. The sacrifice of the Roman Theban Legion is discussed in several articles found at: http://www.jesus-passion.com/ theban_legion.htm

"Dr. Jack Gaines delivers his message the same way he pitched his fast ball for the Boston Red Sox, hard and true. When I caught it, it hurt, but I caught it. Can you handle the TRUTH? If you can, well, welcome to the Big Leagues."

Don Wise
Producer of the best-selling *The Beginner's Bible*,
Developer of the *African Orphan Development Authority*

Jack Gaines

for
speaking
engagements,
books
and
study guides

contact:

HIS PATH
PUBLICATIONS
A DIVISION OF

ForWord, LLC
P.O. Box 9708
Chesapeake,
Virginia
23321

www.hispath.us
jack@hispath.us